W9-AAE-000

YOU CAN HEAR
GOD'S VOICE

YOU CAN HEAR
GOD'S VOICE

SUPERNATURAL KEYS TO WALKING IN
FELLOWSHIP WITH YOUR HEAVENLY FATHER

KEVIN L. ZADAI

© Copyright 2020–Kevin L. Zadai

Printed in the United States of America. All rights reserved. No portion of this book may be reproduced, stored in a retrieval system, or transmitted in any form or by any means—electronic, mechanical, photocopy, recording, scanning, or other—except for brief quotations in critical reviews or articles, without the prior written permission of the publisher. Unless otherwise identified, Scripture quotations are taken from the New King James Version. Copyright © 1982 by Thomas Nelson, Inc. Used by permission. All rights reserved. Scripture quotations marked AMP are taken from the Amplified® Bible, Copyright © 2015 by The Lockman Foundation, La Habra, CA 90631. All rights reserved. Used by permission. Scripture quotations marked KJV are taken from the King James Version. Scripture quotations marked TPT are taken from *The Passion Translation*, Copyright © 2014, 2015, 2016, 2017, www.thepassiontranslation.com. Used by permission of BroadStreet Publishing Group, LLC, Racine, Wisconsin, USA. All rights reserved. Scripture quotations marked NLT are taken from the Holy Bible, New Living Translation, copyright 1996, 2004, 2015. Used by permission of Tyndale House Publishers, Wheaton, Illinois 60189. All rights reserved. All emphasis within Scripture quotations is the author's own.

Published by Harrison House Publishers
Shippensburg, PA 17257

Cover design by Eileen Rockwell
Interior design by Terry Clifton

ISBN 13 TP: 978-1-6803-1513-4
ISBN 13 eBook: 978-1-6803-1514-1
ISBN 13 HC: 978-1-6803-1516-5
ISBN 13 LP: 978-1-6803-1515-8

For Worldwide Distribution, Printed in the U.S.A.
3 4 5 6 7 8 / 24 23 22 21 20

DEDICATION

I dedicate this book to the Lord Jesus Christ. When I died during surgery and met with Jesus on the other side, He insisted I return to life on the earth and help people with their destinies. Because of Jesus' love and concern for people, the Lord has actually chosen to send a person back from death to help everyone who will receive that help so that his or her destiny and purpose is secure in Him. I want You, Lord, to know that when You come to take me to be with You someday, it is my sincere hope that people remember not me but the revelation of Jesus Christ that You have revealed through me. I want others to know that I am merely being obedient to Your heavenly calling and mission, which is to reveal Your plan for the fulfillment of the divine destiny for each of God's children.

ACKNOWLEDGMENTS

In addition to sharing my story with everyone through the books *Heavenly Visitation: A Guide to the Supernatural; Days of Heaven on Earth: A Guide to the Days Ahead; A Meeting Place with God; Your Hidden Destiny Revealed; Praying from the Heavenly Realms: Supernatural Secrets to a Lifestyle of Answered Prayer; The Agenda of Angels: What the Holy Ones Want You to Know About the Next Move of God*, the Lord gave me a commission to produce this book, *You Can Hear God's Voice*. This book addresses some of the revelations concerning the areas that Jesus reviewed and revealed to me through the Word of God and by the Spirit of God during several visitations. I want to thank everyone who has encouraged me, assisted me, and prayed for me during the writing of this work, especially my spiritual parents, Dr. Jesse Duplantis and Dr. Cathy Duplantis. Special thanks to my wonderful wife, Kathi, for her love and dedication to the Lord and to me. Thank you, Sid Roth and staff, for your love of our supernatural Messiah Jesus. Thank you, Warrior Notes staff, for the wonderful job editing this book. Thank you, Harrison House Publishers for your support of this project. Special thanks, as well, to all my friends who know that God wants us to hear His voice and lead us into the next move of God's Spirit!

CONTENTS

INTRODUCTION

HEARING GOD'S VOICE IS SUCH AN IMPORTANT PART OF any Christian's walk with God. It enhances everything in life and keeps the believer hand in hand with the Creator of the universe, providing fellowship, guidance, protection and so much more.

I have always desired to have this deep, personal relationship with my Creator even though I was not made aware of that possibility until I was nineteen years old. A coworker mentioned that I needed to be born again so I could enjoy a personal relationship with Jesus. I remember asking God for this relationship and promising I would serve Him if I could have that same personal relationship the people in the Bible had with their Creator.

Over the past forty years of walking with God, I have gleaned an amazing amount of wisdom concerning the voice of God. It is out of this experience I share the precepts in this book with you.

May the voice of the Lord in your life continually have predominance as you mature into the sons and daughters of the Most High God we were all designed to become.

—KEVIN L. ZADAI, TH.D.

Chapter 1

HIS VOICE IN THE SECRET PLACE

When you sit enthroned under the shadow of Shaddai,
you are hidden in the strength of God Most High.
—Psalm 91:1 TPT

WITHOUT A DOUBT, EVERY ONE OF US NEEDS MORE REV-elation about the secret place where we are invited to dwell. In fact, God desires for us to know more about it, and He has asked me to share with you the importance of hearing His voice and understanding the environment He has provided for you. Because of God's knowledge and understanding of you and your needs, He has provided the secret place for you to dwell hidden in His strength and protection, safe from an oftentimes evil, harsh world.

Notice again, our text Scripture that says, *"When you sit enthroned under the shadow of Shaddai, you are hidden in the strength of God Most High.*" Did you catch that word, *enthroned?* Jesus said that those who overcome will sit with Him on a throne (see Revelation 3:21).

Let's continue through Psalm 91 noticing words and phrases and understanding their meanings:

> *He's the hope that holds me and the Stronghold to shelter me, the only God for me, and my great confidence. He will rescue you from every hidden trap of the enemy, and he will protect you from false accusation and any deadly curse.*
>
> —PSALM 91:2-3 TPT

In these verses, the psalmist describes the benefits of making the Father's shadow our dwelling place—not just a place to visit or a drive-thru window. The problem is that we tend to create our own version of the Bible based on our experiences. When things do not happen the way we think they should, we automatically trim down the Word and airbrush it so we can deal with what seem to be discrepancies. But it is foolishness to take away from the power of God just because we have not experienced it in its fullness.

None of the Israelites experienced God in His power except Moses because he chose to go up to meet with God (see Exodus 33). He chose to listen to the Lord when everyone else said no. The Israelites were afraid because they did not have a relationship with God. They looked at the fire, they heard the thunder and the lightning, they saw the dark cloud, and ultimately, they threw Moses under the bus. They said, "You go up. We know you're not coming back, so we are just going to build a calf and worship it and be crazy people." Even though they had left Egypt, they carried Egypt in their hearts.

Twice Moses went up the mountain and spent forty days with Jesus and learned God's ways. After these encounters, Moses decided there were some things God was holding back, so we find in Scripture that Moses' vocabulary shifts as he pursues God.

In Exodus 33:15, Moses tells God that he would not go forth unless God would send His presence. The word he uses is *paniym*, which means "faces" and relates to God as a triune being. Later in verse 18, we see the shift where Moses insists that God show him His glory. Here he uses the word *kabowd*, which means "weighty glory" and is actually God's personality that surrounds Him in the throne room. You encounter God's personality before you even get to Him because in the glory is everything God is—that which cannot be spoken, cannot be written, and cannot be explained.

I can speak from experience about God's almost indescribably astounding glory. At age 31, during a routine surgery, myself on the "other side of the veil" with Jesus in a heavenly visitation that forever marked my life. I learned so much about the Kingdom of God and the glory of God.

If you get in that glory and there is anything wrong with you, it will not be wrong any longer. That is why I did not want to leave Heaven, especially the throne room because that is the seat of power and where God's personality invades the whole area. In the glory there are no questions, no disease, and no limitations. In the glory, you do not have to try to be you, you simply *are* you. In the glory, no one will confront you or hurt you because the glory corrects anything that is wrong. It is in this secret place of God that you were created to dwell, and it's where you learn to hear God's voice and understand His ways—His very personality.

THE FORCE OF THE GLORY

The Word never says that angels have wings except for the seraphim and the cherubim. The cherubim that are in the throne room are huge and have wings because they cover God's glory so those around Him can withstand it. There is a shadow cast even though there is not a shadow in Heaven.

This glory is even beyond light because it is who God is. Everything about God is beyond anything you know. We would never be walking on this earth in pride if we actually had that revelation. There would never be a reason to promote ourselves. In the throne room, the cherubim are literally guarding God, protecting everything around Him from the full force of the glory emanating from His face.

That shadow is what Moses is talking about in this Psalm. We are to stand in the shadow of the Almighty—the shadow created by the wings of the cherubim that provide cover.

When Moses was in the cleft of the rock, he had understanding because he saw God walk by and heard Him announce His name and personality. Moses realized that in this glory no sickness can dwell, no demon can harm, and no wrong can happen. Moses wrote Psalm 91 from that revelation of God's weighty glory.

His massive arms are wrapped around you, protecting you. You can run under his covering of majesty and hide. His arms of faithfulness are a shield keeping you from harm.

—Psalm 91:4 TPT

Moses was a real man who encountered real glory and wrote about his experience. This Scripture is very anointed, but it seems impossible if you measure it up to your own experiences. Remember that it is truth even if it does not happen in your life. It is where you are going, and you have to enforce that truth every day. That is what the Lord wants for you and what He is telling me to share. He is telling you to let Him wrap His arms around you and protect you. He is telling you that He is covering you with His majesty and you can hide in that majesty. He has arms of faithfulness, and He is a shield, keeping you from harm.

You will never worry about an attack of demonic forces at night nor have to fear a spirit of darkness coming against you.

—Psalm 91:5 TPT

No demon can come near you if you are in the shadow of the cherubim's wings.

Even in a time of disaster, with thousands and thousands being killed, you will remain unscathed and unharmed. You will be a spectator as the wicked perish in judgment, for they will be paid back for what they have done! When we live

our lives within the shadow of God Most High,
our secret hiding place, we will always be shielded
from harm. How then could evil prevail against
us or disease infect us?

—Psalm 91:7-10 TPT

THE CORRECTIVE NATURE
OF THE SECRET PLACE

Moses is experiencing this protective covering, and he realizes that nothing can kill him. He was so convinced of it that when he reached 120 years old and was not allowed to go into the Promised Land, God took him up to the mountain and Moses fell dead before the Lord. The Lord had to tell him it was time for him to pass away and be with Him. Scripture says that he died in perfect health. It is possible for human beings to be so overcome, overwhelmed, and convinced of who God is that God has to tell them to die or they will not. In Genesis, God had set a limit of 120 years due to the fall.

I realize that everything in my life that needs correcting has to be turned over to the secret place. He has to win me over to the point where all my doubts and fears are driven out, and I have a new script for my life—a new plan and a new map. The new plan is based on His ability and not my inabilities; it is based on what God says. For example, if God says you will be married, then you will be married. It does not matter if you do not have a date because God speaks those things that are not as though they were (see Romans 4:17).

Are you beginning to see why it is so important that you dwell in the secret place—in the very glory of God? The secret place is where you encounter God and He speaks wonderful things to your life. He is in your future, and He is speaking it as though it is your now. If you make the Most High your dwelling place, you become in sync with Him, and you start to live and move and have your being in Him (see Acts 17:28).

Then things start to happen that appear to be favor. It may even get out of control and people may get mad because they are jealous and want what you have. But they must pay the price by getting in the secret place for themselves. Many believers are wondering how to hear God's voice. My first question will always be, how much time are you spending in the secret place? That's where God is dwelling right now! That's where you encounter the glory.

To be honest with you, some people's heads might be too big to fit into the secret place; they might have to downsize a little bit. They may be "cross Christians," who are still at the cross. The president of the college that I graduated from once said, "If Christians are still at the cross, then they are cross with everybody." You have to go up and be seated with Jesus in the heavenly realms. You have to go into the secret place and let everything that does not belong there anymore stay on the outside. When you are in the secret place, you do not need those things that you have been dependent on. You do not need them because God's voice is far above and exceedingly beyond what you could ever think (see Ephesians 3:20). I have experienced this, and it's available to you!

Nobody loves me the way that He does. No one has cared for me the way that He did when I was with Him. I have never met anyone who loved me as much as He did. He is wrapped up in me and thinks I am the best thing that has ever happened. When I came back to the earth, I had to realize that no one else got the email that I had gotten about being His favorite. But here's the real truth: we are all His favorites!

God wraps Himself up in you, He adores you, and He is in relentless pursuit of you. God wants you to come to this secret place because He wants to win you over. He wants to love on you, and it is time to receive His love. He wants to share wonderful things with you about your life. It is time to let Him love on you. It is time to be loved and not just love. It is time to receive from God. This would fix a lot of your "giving buttons" that are broken because you need to learn to first receive.

When I was in the secret place, the Lord looked right in and locked eyes with me. He believed in me because I came from Him. When I looked into His eyes, I saw that everything about my life was wrapped up in His heart before I even came into existence. He made the universes for you and me to enjoy.

The assignment I have for the rest of my life is to get people to not only encounter the secret place but to live there. When that happens, there will be a movement toward God, and that movement toward God will be a movement toward the lost, and we will pull people in and teach them about the love of God.

SOLUTIONS, NOT SIN

It is interesting that people say I do not speak often about sin. Yet, Jesus told me to come back and give people the solution. If all I do is talk about sin or talk about problems, then after a while I will need you to pray for me! I believe that if you have begun reading this book, then you expect to hear solutions. If I start testifying about all the bad stuff that has happened to me in my life then we will forget why we are here, and we lose sight of what God has promised us. In your life, you must emphasize what God says is the truth, and just go there and make that your world. Do not worry about the evil around you, simply choose to change it. That is why we have to be involved with our towns, our cities, our states, and our countries. We need to be involved because we *do* make a difference, and God does have a voice through us that wins people over to Him.

Through the Holy Spirit, you are the hands, the feet and voice of God on the earth, and you are to function as such through the church. You need to have an abiding place where your whole environment is wrapped up in the God who is wrapped up in you. I was amazed at how many things were told to me when I was in Heaven that I would never have accepted while I was in my body and in the flesh because my mind was not able to receive it. There are so many people in Heaven who are excited and blessed by your life on earth when you are faithful.

GRATITUDE AND GIVING

The Father loves when you are thankful. When something good happens to you, thank God for it. He secretly tells angels to do things for you and then waits to see if you will acknowledge Him. Sometimes you will find that you have been blessed with more than one of something because one of them might be earmarked for someone else. I know everything I receive is a gift from God. Sometimes the Holy Spirit will lead me to give it away and tell me, "That was never yours." You see, I was just a carrier of it until the proper time that I handed it over to the owner. I look at everything in my life this way. When God gives me a word, it is not just for me, it is a word for the whole body. When I made money at my job, the Lord would tell me what I was supposed to do with it. As I responded to the Lord's voice in our giving, Kathi and I got out of debt. People would come to us and say, "I want to pay off your house." We have had two houses paid off now, and the one we are in now was already paid off.

Right now, your environment has to change. You have to begin to frame your world by the Word of God and become accustomed to the personality of God which is in the glory. You can hear God's voice, but it is in this place of secrecy where He is a tower, and you are protected, and He begins to talk to you about how much He loves you.

Most people will sit in the secret place and what they hear will be too much for them. It may be too much for you too because it will not be like anything you have ever heard. I have a show on Sid Roth's network (ISN) called "The Secret Place." I named it this because everyone wants to be safe and everyone wants to have value. In this secret place with the Lord, you will know your value and feel safe. It is a place that God has provided for us; it is supernatural, and you can access it right now. If I ever feel sick, I go to the secret place because I know the disease cannot dwell there. God cannot fail, and it is impossible for Him to lie, so if He is for you, then who can be against you?

We must begin to understand the shift that must happen in our lives and in this generation. We have to change the way we see things. We need to be in the secret place and make that our vantage point.

So much is pulling on us down here on the earth. I need the restoration of the secret place to be able to do what I do. Recently while in Switzerland, I preached at twenty-five services in two weeks, which amounted to approximately fifty hours of teaching. Immediately when I got home, I switched bags and went to Australia for another ten days. There, I preached three times a day, plus I took out the witch covens and the masons while I was there! What I am trying to tell you is that there are no limitations to your productivity. When I returned home from several weeks abroad, it was as though I had not preached in three months; I was completely recovered. This is what happens to you when you live in the secret place.

Like Moses, I want to get to the place where God has to tell me to die and come to Heaven at one hundred and twenty years old because I keep living a long life, supernaturally! I have to shift my perception so that I see the world from the eyes of Jesus with compassion.

People do not bring me down, rather, I bring them up. If they cannot handle it, they go away from me. You must set the bar. You must be excellent in this life and do everything with excellence. You are going to succeed in your mission. I would rather go slow and get it done rather than create a mess with my failures; I would rather take my time and do it right the first time.

The perfect plan for this generation is to abide in the secret place to the point that when you go out, people begin to notice that your face is glowing. It happened to Moses. He did not even have the latest Christian worship band singing to him, but he was able to walk in that glory. He did not listen to a well-known TV minister, and yet his face was transformed. People were afraid to look at him because he looked like God. His face had beams coming out of it.

I would rather aim high like this than trip over my own feet because I was looking down. It is time to look up. It is time to let God set the pace for your life and let Him set your goals. Let Him determine the doctrine through His Word because it is all scripted. If I told you how scripted your life is it would be hard for you to accept because it looks so random, which is a tactic of the devil. He sets it up to make your life look and feel random—like failure after failure. But your life is not that at all! The devil does that to get you into a mindset, once you accept it, you unknowingly rewrite doctrine.

You *can* hear God's voice! But you must start to be a good receiver and let the Father love on you. He is going to speak more highly of you than anyone else will. He is going to send angels to help you. The angels are excited to perform miracles in your life and help you line up with the provision God has for your life. He is telling people that it is time to step up a little bit. It is time to see what God really has for you.

God sends angels with special orders to protect you wherever you go, defending you from all harm.
—PSALM 91:11 TPT

The angels defend you from *all* harm. That is their command. If something fails, it is not their fault. There have been times when I was told to wait five minutes before driving away in my car, and then as I drove down the road I drove past an accident where somebody died in the intersection. It only happens a couple of times before you get smart and realize that maybe God is trying to help you—He's trying to speak to you. He doesn't necessarily stop the wreck, but He stops you from being in the wreck. I am not going to be on an airplane that goes down because He has plenty of time to either fix the airplane or reroute me.

When you get to Heaven, you will realize that you were in the right place at the right time because you followed Him daily. Your life is all coordinated, and the angels are all around right now excited to help you walk into your destiny. In these last days, spending time in the secret place will not only cause you to overcome in your own life, but everywhere you go people will get healed by your shadow and healed by your smile. That's why living in the secret place is so vital to not only hear God's voice but obey and follow through with what you hear. Your whole day—even your whole life—can be rerouted simply by learning to hear God's voice.

THE FULLNESS OF MY SALVATION

If you walk into a trap, they'll be there for you and keep you from stumbling. You'll even walk unharmed among the fiercest powers of darkness, trampling every one of them beneath your feet!
—PSALM 91:12-13 TPT

Jesus pulled from this Scripture when He said, "I give you authority to trample on serpents and scorpions." Jesus knew the Scriptures, and He knew this psalm.

For here is what the Lord has spoken to me:

"Because you have delighted in me as my great lover, I will greatly protect you. I will set you in a high place, safe and secure before my face. I will answer your cry for help every time you pray, and you will find and feel my presence even in your time of pressure and trouble. I will be your glorious hero and give you a feast. You will be satisfied with a full life and with all that I do for you. For you will enjoy the fullness of my salvation!"
—PSALM 91:14-16 TPT

At the end of this verse, the word *salvation* has been translated from the original Hebrew word *yĕshuw'ah*, which is literally *Jesus.* So really, God is saying, "You will enjoy the fullness of my Jesus."

Do you realize that this secret place has always been there? Yet, if I had not gone to Heaven, I would not have known how powerful this place is. Now I want to go there often because this world is so broken that the only way I can be effective in this life is to go and spend some time with my heavenly Father. I go to the secret place and talk to Him, and He talks to me and brings correction. He tells me, "No, this is not how I feel about you," and He shares instead what He knows about me. "This is what I know about you," He says. "This is what I am doing for you, and you need to receive it." In this secret place, you sit and receive from your Father so you have something to give out to others.

RECEIVING FRESH MANNA

The biggest problem with ministry and with Christians is that they have nothing to give out because they have not been in the secret place. As a result, they do not have fresh manna. I have been shown the future in the secret place. I know what is going on, and all I have to do is walk it out, and everything becomes synchronized. You get in the secret place and you can watch the future play out before you.

Jesus told me that when He was in the secret place alone on a mountain, it was there that He was shown the "films of tomorrow." He was shown visions of what the Pharisees would say to Him and who would be coming to Him in need of healing. He was shown what He was supposed to talk about. Jesus was operating as a man, and He had to be fully dependent upon God. He was displaying how our relationship is supposed to be with God.

In the secret place, God will speak to you, but you must frame your world with the Word of God because He is going to speak out mysteries and speak out the future. You must be able to fully receive what it is that God is speaking to you from the glory. What He speaks to you will be completely life changing. It will be so good that you will be healed and set free. You will feel and hear your sicknesses leave. This was God's plan for the children of Israel, but they did not come up to the mountain. However, in His mercy, God told Moses to build a tabernacle of meeting and invite Israel and He would come meet with them there. The only two people who showed up were Joshua and Moses. Joshua was the only person who qualified to lead Israel. Abiding in the secret place is the key. This is how you become part of what God is doing on the earth. You must take the time to let God shift your perception.

From this point forward, your life is going to start to be framed from your destiny that was written before you were born. The angels will come and help you. They are sent to build scenarios and replicate what is in Heaven. Everything that has been given to you has been given in order to implement what God is doing; you will receive the assistance of the angels to accomplish it.

For example, God wants us to get out of the poverty and debt mentality. He does not want us to be in debt. Jesus told me that not only does He not want me to be in debt but He does not even want me to see a bill. I asked the Lord how to do that, and He told me to pay my bills in advance. I pay all my bills years in advance, and I do not even have to look at bills coming in.

I want to encourage people not to filter out Scripture in order to make it more palatable for what they are going through.

The Jesus I met is never going to be compromised; He is never going to lower the standard to make someone feel better. People come against prosperity because they do not understand that there is a biblical prosperity that has to do with *provision* for your *vision;* it is about the Kingdom of God, and it has to do with the harvest. You are a steward because you can be trusted, but there are many people who do not pass their money test, and God cannot trust them.

God has no needs except to spend time with us. Our heavenly Father has invested so much in order for us to be brought back to Him, and all He wants is our time and our smile. God wants us to let Him love on us, and yet, it is the last thing that we do. As sons and daughters, we have qualified to be ambassadors for Him, and He will take care of us. God couldn't care less about what people think about it; it is called favor. God favors people because they have let Him win them over.

Walking in the Timeless Realm

At the end of this age, we will be walking into a place only few individuals have ever experienced. Moses and Enoch walked into this place; it was a timeless realm, and it became their normal. Enoch never experienced death, and Moses had to be told to experience it. In his fallen state, Adam lived 930 years. Your heavenly Father desires to come and talk with you, but His voice might come as a whisper to you. You can hear His voice but you may have to be ready to hear what He will say as a still small voice. This whisper may have revelation beyond what you can handle in your mind.

PROTECTING THE SECRET PLACE

We have allowed deception, and it has allowed a shift in our perception and reality. For instance, our culture has made abortion acceptable, but if you were to disrupt an eagle's nest, you would be sent to prison. Jesus came to give us life and life more abundantly. He did not come to take a life. Christianity has become counterculture, and now you must push these things out and change your perception back. Don't allow your secret place to be invaded.

I had to die, go to Heaven, and then come back to see what was available to me in the tent of meeting, where God's glory is. He changes my perception and my false ideas. Likewise, God has been trying to speak things to you, but you have not been able to understand it and limited yourself as a result. I believe right now by the power of God that He wants your borders to fall in a favorable way. I sense that angels are ready and standing by to assist you. David said, the boundaries have fallen in a favorable place (see Psalm 16:6). God is helping us by taking the tent pegs up, taking up the border pegs, and expanding our borders.

Lord, let the borders fall where You want them to fall. May they be limitless. Increase our capacity to receive from You right now. It is a gift! Receive it now!

Prayer of Revelation and Understanding

> *Father, I thank You for the secret place. I thank You that You want to reveal Your ways. I hunger and thirst after You, and I desire to know You. I ask the Holy Spirit to come and counsel me and*

take me up and into the spirit world where there is revelation and understanding. Father, I repent for my unbelief. I realize that You have so much more. I repent, and I ask You to forgive me and take my borders to where they should be. Help me to be strong and be of good courage as I go forth to see Your Kingdom reign. Hallelujah!

A STORY

I remember having the glory of Father God visiting me in my office for weeks at a time. I would sit in my special chair to write, and it was as though a spiritual cloud would come in and God would visit me for sometimes hours at a time. This went on for several months and God would speak to me in His secret place, which had become my office.

Many powerful revelations came out of this time. The Lord's voice was so sweet, even though it was just a still, small voice. He would tell me I was loved and valued. I remember Him telling me I was healed. Shortly after this, I found out that I did not need to wear my contact lenses any longer. After going to the optometrist, I found that my eyes had improved considerably and was told that there was now almost no need for corrective lenses. Still, to this day I do not need them, and it has been several years since I heard the whisper that I was healed.

You will need to sit quietly in an environment that becomes the secret place of the Most High. Then, allow Him to confirm His Word to you as He whispers truth to you. It will change your life!

Chapter 2

THE SOUND OF HIS VOICE

*Proclaim his majesty, all you mighty
champions, you sons of Almighty God, giving
all the glory and strength back to him!*
—PSALM 29:1 TPT

PSALM 29 IS DESCRIBING THE VOICE OF THE LORD AND the force of His strength. Yet even in His mighty majesty, He speaks to us in a gentle whisper, because we are His sons and daughters. I want you to see who our Father is: He is an all-powerful, almighty God, and He chooses to meet with you and whisper to you in the secret place. We have a privilege of being called children of God and sons of God.

*For the earnest expectation of the creation eagerly
waits for the revealing of the sons of God. For the*

creation was subjected to futility, not willingly, but because of Him who subjected it in hope; because the creation itself also will be delivered from the bondage of corruption into the glorious liberty of the children of God. For we know that the whole creation groans and labors with birth pangs together until now.

—ROMANS 8:19-22

Romans 8 tells us we are now at the end of the age when all creation is groaning for the sons of God to be revealed. The apostle Paul teaches us that as sons of God, we are led by the Spirit of God and can hear God's voice no matter how soft or loud it is. We have a spirit of adoption within us that cries out, "Father, Father" (see Romans 8:15).

We know that God has different ways of speaking to His children. Psalm 29:1 tells us to, "Proclaim his majesty all you mighty champions." David is telling us to proclaim the Lord's majesty and calls us champions. The sons of the Almighty God are champions, and we are to give all the glory and strength back to Him. You are to realize that you are God's ambassador on this earth, and therefore, it is necessary for Him to talk to you.

Notice that the verse does not call us victims! Understand that there is a place where God dwells; and if we go there, we won't want to come back. He is so irresistible, and everything about Him is excellent. He considers us champions—mighty men and women of God. He calls us sons and daughters. Jesus bought us back to sonship with the Father, and we give that glory and strength back to Him in worship.

> *Be in awe before his majesty. Be in awe before such power and might! Come worship wonderful Yahweh, arrayed in all his splendor, bowing in worship as he appears in the beauty of holiness. Give him the honor due his name. Worship him wearing the glory-garments of your holy, priestly calling!*
>
> —Psalm 29:2 TPT

We can just imagine this right now, just as Isaiah saw Him high and lifted up with the train of His robe filling the temple. Isaiah saw wonderful things happening in the throne room, but he felt undone or lost and doomed because of the glory. He saw the splendor and the majesty of God Almighty and fell (see Isaiah 6:1-5).

I have experienced this majesty. I saw saints and angels falling down, and those who sat in the front row of the throne room could not handle the fullness of the glory. I saw fire and glory. There was gold in the air, and it was swirling all around. The breath of all the saints manifested as a gold mist that was coming and washing over God the Father and God the Son. As the saints praised, Heaven began to shake and vibrate. The unity of the combined voices was so strong and powerful that it caused the air to ignite and become a river of life. It became liquid diamonds that had melted; it looked like diamonds, and yet, it was all water. There is so much going on in the throne room, and everything that has breath is praising the Lord. He appears in all His holy beauty, and we give Him honor. We are given glory-garments and made holy priests of the Most High God.

We need to be in this type of worship so that we can hear God's voice. In this atmosphere, we give Him praise and honor, wearing our glory garments. He then speaks back to us as His sons and daughters, a mighty priesthood.

HIS VOICE ECHOES

The voice of the Lord echoes through the skies and seas. The Glory-God reigns as he thunders in the clouds. So powerful is his voice, so brilliant and bright, how majestic as he thunders over the great waters!

—PSALM 29:3-4 TPT

God has such a powerful voice it can sound like thunder. In fact, we read about God's voice thundering many times as He reveals Himself throughout Scripture. We read about it on Mount Sinai when the mountain was on fire and the people heard thunder. When God spoke from Heaven, some said it had thundered (see Exodus 19:16 and John 12:29).

His tympanic thunder topples the strongest of trees. His symphonic sound splinters the mighty forests. Now he moves Zion's mountains by the might of his voice, shaking the snowy peaks with his earsplitting sound! The lightning-fire flashes, striking as he speaks.

—PSALM 29:5-7 TPT

God's voice is so strong it moves mountains! As you think about what you face, the challenges that stand before you, and the attacks of the enemy, just remember that God's voice can level mountains and splinter forests. His thunder can topple trees. Remember, too, that the same voice is also inside of you, crying out, "Abba Father." As sons and daughters of God, we have the Holy Spirit crying out within us. We are adopted by the Most High God. We are His children, and He is speaking on our behalf.

> *Lord, you are my secret hiding place, protecting me from these troubles, surrounding me with songs of gladness! Your joyous shouts of rescue release my breakthrough.*
>
> —Psalm 32:7 TPT

God is your Warrior, and He sings over you with songs of deliverance. When He reveals Himself to you, the earth cracks; fault lines are formed, and there is shaking because He speaks with His voice. When you realize the power of His voice, your perception of who He is will begin to be framed. You will begin to have a revelation about how big He is and how strong His voice can be. Even with the enormity and power of His voice, He is able to speak as a father speaks to his children. He whispers to you and speaks calming things through the Holy Spirit inside of you.

> *God reveals himself when he makes the fault lines quake, shaking deserts, speaking his voice. God's mighty voice makes the deer to give birth. His thunderbolt voice lays the forest bare. In his*

> *temple all fall before him with each one shouting,*
> *"Glory, glory, the God of glory!"*
> —PSALM 29:8-9 TPT

During my visit to Heaven, I saw that at the end of the age, meetings were being held and people were encountering the glory. I saw people shouting and crying out, "Glory! Glory! The Father is here! The glory of God is here!" I saw that He was revealing Himself to His people.

> *Above the furious flood, the Enthroned One*
> *reigns, the King-God rules with eternity at his*
> *side. This is the one who gives his strength and*
> *might to his people. This is the Lord giving us his*
> *kiss of peace.*
> —PSALM 29:10-11 TPT

We will see the Enthroned One reigning; the King, our God, will rule. Here, in verse 10, it says that eternity is standing by the Lord's side as a servant. God is not bound by eternity; it stands at His side. This Scripture is encouraging us to realize and concentrate on the fact that our God is the Creator of everything and whatever He says goes. We are His mighty men and women, His sons and daughters. We are His inheritance, His holy priesthood, and we are not bound by eternity either. The Lord showed me that we are supposed to be down here enforcing the blessing and pushing back the curse. We are to be preaching the gospel and letting people know that God is a good God who loves them.

I saw that we are supposed to allow angels to minister for us and to us. They are available to us 24/7 in order to accomplish the will of the Father. In the throne room, I could hear the voice of the Lord rumbling, the saints and the angels singing; Heaven was shaking. We are in the fallen world, but it does not stop what God is doing in the heavenly realms and in the throne room. Remind yourself that God has given you the power to trample on serpents and scorpions (see Luke 10:19), and down here you are to be walking in dominion. Concentrate on the heavenly realms. Set your mind on things above, so you can walk them out here below.

> *Set your mind on things above, not on things on the earth. For you died, and your life is hidden with Christ in God.*
>
> —COLOSSIANS 3:2-3

In Heaven, I saw that there are many realms and, while we are on this earth, we are to walk in the power of those realms. We are to yield to the spirit realm and to our Father who is in Heaven. We are to yield to the angels who have been sent to help us. He is King and Judge, and He is taking care of everything concerning you.

When I was with Jesus, I was given entrance into a room. Within that room, I saw the whole known universe, and it was just a four-inch globe on God's desk! Then I saw myself as a small figure standing on top of the desk. I reached my hands up and formed the shape of a candle; at that point, I caught on fire. I looked up and saw God looking at me adoringly.

You make your messengers into winds of the Spirit
and all your ministers become flames of fire.
—PSALM 104:4 TPT

There is fire in His throne room and fire in His eyes. His angels are flames of fire. Think about the fire of God. He is burning up your enemies in front of you with a consuming fire because He *is* a consuming fire.

ELEMENTS OF GOD

In describing the attributes of God in Psalm 29, the psalmist describes the very elements of the earth as fire, rain, echoes, clouds, and thunder. We are familiar with these elements, and we know their sound and feel. With these words, David does his best to portray the power of God. The descriptions almost sound destructive, but it is because God is so incredibly powerful. Now that the earth is in a fallen state, nothing is flexible and things break. Things deteriorate and die and no longer correspond to God's original intent for them. We may have disappointments down here and things don't always work out perfectly. Your house does not clean itself, and your kids do not behave unless you tell them to. The fallen world is a broken world, and when God comes down, there is a powerful response simply because the world cannot handle His power. I saw that God has to temper Himself when He comes here just so we are comfortable and can bear His presence.

I have encountered these things, and I have heard God's audible voice. It shook the whole house. When you hear His voice, it is not just a small thing. Yet I have also heard Him whisper to me, and I have had Him kiss me from Heaven and not say one word. Through others, He has said and done things for me that no one could have ever known. He moves through other people on your behalf. That is our loving Father! God is merciful, but He also is the powerful, authoritative, Psalm 29 God. In order to help your world be demon free and drama free, you must take this medicine that is Psalm 29 and remind yourself of who your Father is. Remember, one day God will no longer hold back against your enemy. He will fight a war for you and display His power.

I encountered this in Heaven. I encountered the fire in Jesus' eyes. I used to think that I could get away with doing things on my own. I would think, *Maybe God is having a bad day and that is why He told me no about a particular thing.* Jesus appeared to me and told me not to find myself on the wrong side of Him. He said, "I never told you to go there. You know you are to go through Me."

Your heavenly Father disciplines those He loves. He treats you as His child. When you listen to people talk about God, they often only see one side of Him. In fact, you won't see all sides of Him because there are many facets of God. Even the dimensions that God lives in are so many that you would never get them all in this realm because He is literally squeezing, supernaturally His Kingdom into this physical realm through His people. Let me explain. The earthly realm has been downgraded into a few, visible dimensions. For example, in Heaven I saw that music has color, smell, and is multi-dimensional. In Heaven music is alive, but in our dimension we simply hear music. In the same way, everything in Heaven is enhanced, expanded, and multi-dimensional. When God speaks to you, you will have revelation and understanding for years and be able to eat off of His words many times because of the levels of revelation.

All things are working for your good, and you really cannot fail. If you will continue to acknowledge Him in all your ways, He will direct your paths (see Romans 8:28 and Proverbs 3:6). God will help you and discipline you. He is a good Father and desires to come down and visit you. He desires to talk with you through the Holy Spirit and the Word of God.

When believers do not experience God in this way, it is because they don't yield to Him and are likely experiencing warfare. We must be strengthened in our warfare by waging war. We are to proclaim the will of God and the Kingdom of God with our mouths. We are to use the prophecies that we have received and declare the Word of God. We are to pray in the Spirit and bring fire from the altar down to this earth.

We are supposed to yield to the Holy Spirit as we play music and make melody in our hearts. There is music that needs to come into this realm to be released in these last days. People will learn how to yield and play and sing prophetically. God wants to reveal to you the future and begin to show you what is next. He will give you strategies and place ideas into your mind. You will be given His thoughts and begin to think, *What would I do tomorrow if I could not fail?* He will take the limits off of you by changing your mindset. No one in Heaven is limiting you!

THE INTENTION OF GOD'S WORD

We do not always hear God's voice audibly, but He speaks to us just the same. Yet, in this hour of the Church, God is toning down His voice. He is preparing His children for an amazing future and wants to be able to speak us and not have to speak it twice. His whisper can be so powerful that He does not have to increase the volume. I hear the Spirit of God speaking to all of us saying, "I only have to speak once, and it is not going to be repealed to a higher court." There is no one beyond Him; if He says something over you, then that is the end of it. You must get yourself into a place where you can hear His whisper because the potency of the whisper is just like Psalm 29.

The voice of the Lord needs to convince you of how you would live if you could not fail. When you get to that place, you will experience so much favor you will have difficulty remembering a time when something failed. I believe people who are called of God should have everything they need to do what they have been called to do. You should not have to manipulate or work extra. You are supposed to prosper and be in good health. Healing is not for the believer but the lost; believers should walk in divine health because Jesus healed everyone.

I am willing to let God expand my world—let Him unfold who He is and have His way in my world. We all must be willing to let this happen. It will shift the way we see everything. It does not take much for God to shift our environments and our perceptions, but we have to let Him take us to a vantage point where we see things the way He sees them. That means that just because He is holding back His intensity when He talks, does not mean that what He is saying is any less potent. God is really protecting us by not speaking in full force.

You have to move into the other realm because if you start to interpret through the lens of this realm, you will miss all the realms and dimensions God was speaking from. If you want to have miracles and manifestations, then you must allow God to interpret what He says. When He visits you and tells you that He loves you, there are multiple levels of understanding. He is saying that He wrote your book, and He thought of you. He put you in your mother's womb, and now He is nurturing you. When He says that He loves you, He is speaking from the place where He first formed you and the place where you will one day present yourself to Him and give an account for your life. Everything that God says is based on that entire cycle.

THE SONS OF GOD REVEALED

The sons of God have begun to be unveiled, but it will take a while for everyone to jump in and understand. Enoch did not notify people that he was crossing over and visiting with God. The prophets are seen as heroes in the next generation, but while they are alive, many people want to kill them because they speak from the other realm.

God needs His children to have answers and be able to take care of things; and we are to qualify at the highest level of excellence. God wants to impart what He has into people, and when that happens, they become sons and daughters. God births people, and they are His; He has a destiny for each generation. In this generation, we do not want to be robbed anymore.

THE WHISPER OF HIS VOICE

The predominant way that God leads us is by the still small voice. I have heard God's audible voice, but it was not with my ears. His voice shook my whole being. I heard it as though my whole body was an ear. I cannot hear God's voice for you. You need to check in with your Father for yourself. You need to check in with the Spirit of God, and you need to be friends with Jesus. Through this book, I am teaching you to position yourself to hear the still small voice. There are stages of how God does things, but He speaks to us in the innermost part of us. I found that the best way to hear the still small voice within us is to spend time alone apart from any of the input from the world so God can lead and guide you.

I have been walking with the Lord for 40 years, and I've learned that if I am unsure of what God is saying to me, it is all right. I can always go to the Word of God for guidance. A majority of my guidance comes from reading His Word. The Word of God speaks to me and helps my prayer time because it causes me to know the boundaries of His ways. When I pray, I know that I will receive what I have asked for because I know the truth of His Word.

PLACE YOURSELF IN THE SCRIPTURES

What would you do if you could not fail? This should not be a new concept, but it is. I have seen something on the other side, and it has become my new normal. To everyone else, this concept is still foreign. When Paul talked, he had to be careful about what he said because people were not ready for it. He wanted to go further, but people were still hooked on the milk of the Word (see 1 Corinthians 3:2). I have found myself needing to be patient, and for a long time, I have been consulting with people who are above me on how to release what God has revealed to me.

Much of the church is still drinking milk, and few people actually grasp the Scripture in its fullness. When people read a Scripture, they want to believe it, but it is just too much because they realize what is happening in their lives. They know that if they step out in faith, they could be proven wrong. They become concerned Satan will attack them.

What would happen, though, if God convinces you of who He is and asks you this question: How would you live tomorrow if you could not fail? The Lord asked me to place myself in the Bible and look at every verse as though it is for me. You cannot fail if you meditate on the Word of God in this way. What I do is take on the Scriptures as my own experience, even if it is just in my imagination. I start by imagining what it would be like to be in the Bible. I see myself as Jesus' disciple, as His favorite follower. I imagine Jesus laying His hands on me after a hard day of ministry work. I imagine myself saying, "No, You do not have to lay hands on me; just speak a word," Jesus would love to hear that. I look in the Bible and find out what it is that God likes, and then I do that. Do you now see that when you place yourself in Scripture like this, you hear from God in a whole new way?

I want to find out about the God who is so powerful that when He enters a place it just breaks and, at the same time, He whispers to us in love and makes us His friends. God wants to talk to us in order to get us involved with what He is doing. When we look in the Word, we can see that there were only a few people that God did this with. David wrote Psalm 8, and yet, it says that he was God's friend. You will notice that the people who were visited by God—Abraham, Moses, David, and Enoch—were all considered friends of God.

What is it about God that He is attracted to us? Why is He concerned? Why does He even take notice of us?

> *When I consider Your heavens, the work of Your fingers, the moon and the stars, which You have ordained,* **what is man that You are mindful of him, and the son of man that You visit him?** *For You have made him a little lower than the angels, and You have crowned him with glory and honor. You have made him to have dominion over the works of Your hands; You have put all things under his feet.*
>
> —PSALM 8:3-6

Many believe that this psalm was written from the viewpoint of an angel, asking, "What is man that you are mindful of him?" The angels do not understand salvation. They do not understand why God is so focused on us, but it is because we are made in His image.

God loves you, and He whispers to you so that you can withstand His force. When He speaks to you out of intimacy and tells you that you cannot fail, then you begin to believe His words over you. You begin to frame your world by it and begin to ask yourself, "What *would* I do if I could not fail?"

The angels around you do not think about failure, and the Holy Spirit who is within you does not talk about failure because there is none. When God speaks, He is holding back His power so you can handle it, but He does not hold back what He believes. If He believes that you cannot fail, then what needs to happen to get you into an environment where you can grow, mature, and feel safe?

While He was on the earth, Jesus told people that He was going to die and rise again on the third day, but how many people were waiting for Him on that day? He also told His followers that if they wanted any part of Him, they would have to deny themselves, pick up their cross, and follow Him. No one knew that Jesus was going to die on a cross; everyone around Him thought that He was going to push Rome out and become king of Jerusalem and Israel.

It's the same situation in our day. God is saying things that are beyond our ability to grasp at the time. However, God can give you the ability to grasp His intention; His Word can have its full force on you without Him breaking the cedars and causing earthquakes to happen (Psalm 29). He pulls that back, but He does not pull back the power of His Word because it is truth. God is always speaking to us.

TAKING OFF THE LIMITATIONS

Jesus told us that nothing would be impossible for us if we believe (see Mark 9:23). Therefore, the limitations in our minds need to be taken off. I do this by positioning myself to hear that mighty, powerful voice of the Lord, and I began to sense that through me He wants to say, "Mountain be removed." He wants to be able to speak through us with a command from Heaven. He wants us to tell the demons to leave. It is our responsibility as ambassadors of Heaven to drive out demons and tell the devil, "No!" We are meant to make the devil the victim, pushing him out of the way. The devil is the victim, and we are the victors.

Hearing God's voice brings us out of a victim mentality in every area of our lives. We are supposed to walk in divine health. We should not ever need healing, because we are walking in supernatural health. We are supposed to continually have our needs being met so we have more than enough for others as well as for ourselves. We cannot be selfish and just think that prosperity is for us. We must be Kingdom-minded and know that God wants to get lots of wealth through our hands so we can give to others, help others, and help bring in the harvest in this end time.

We are in the age of grace right now, and God is pouring out His Spirit on all flesh. However, in this age of grace, we must discern that the limitations have been taken off so that we can proclaim the goodness of God to this generation. Determine today to stop living with a victim mentality. We must listen to His voice through His gentle whispers and through His Word regarding areas in our lives where we have given in to a victim mentality. In the midst of hearing His voice, we will also hear the whispers of His love over us as His beloved sons or daughters.

God has a personality, and He likes certain things. When Jesus encountered people who were doing things He liked, He celebrated them. In Matthew 8:5-8, Jesus complimented the centurion for his faith after the centurion told Jesus he understood authority and knew that Jesus only needed to speak the word and his servant would be healed.

We need to get a revelation about God's authority and get to the place that when God speaks His Word over us, we say, "That is enough, it is all that we need!" In Mark 9:23, a man asked Jesus if He was willing to heal. The truth is, we already are healed because from where He is standing we have not yet become sick. When God spoke to us there was no mention of sickness. His divine plan is for us to walk in health. But down here in this world, we judge everything by our experience and miss out on what God is doing in our lives. God is standing in our futures and speaking to us, but it sounds like it is our now.

Jesus told the man in Mark 9, "If you can believe, all things *are* possible to him who believes." Jesus placed it right back into the person's lap and gave him the responsibility and accountability to believe. Jesus is telling us that nothing is impossible. He has taken off all limitations!

When God talks to you, it will be as a spirit being because you are a spirit who has a soul and lives in a body. God is also a spirit, and those who worship Him must worship Him in spirit and truth (see John 4:23). Therefore, God will speak to you Spirit to spirit, but He speaks from a realm with no limitations. He does not doubt Himself. God speaks to you from the authority that framed the world, the same authority that formed you in your mother's womb. He thought of you, He saw you, and He watched you being formed. That is the God we serve. This is the God I saw in Heaven, who brought me back when I almost died. He is a very powerful and knows what He wants.

God had intentions for you, and you must allow God to interpret them. When He speaks, let Him tell you what the intention of His heart is for you. Let him interpret your dreams and interpret His Word. You can walk in authority and dominion, but you need to have understanding. When you want to hear God's voice, you must remember that you are under authority and whatever God says goes. When He speaks, you must be obedient and submit to it. It is important to allow the authority of what He is saying to come into you and enforce His Word and His will for you.

HIS WILL UNVEILED

The voice and will of God are being revealed, and He is teaching us how to hear. Out of revelation, we begin proclaiming His will. Angels are listening to hear what we say because they are sent to accomplish what God has already proclaimed. If we speak His will, then they have permission as well because we are speaking the very will of God from Heaven. God always proclaims the end from the beginning because He is in a timeless realm. He can speak through prophets, and they can proclaim things that have not even happened yet. God can speak the very end from the beginning. He is the Author and Finisher of our faith.

Do not hesitate, but let God have His way with you. Tell Him, "Lord, I want Your perfect will." Get to know what He says in His Word, and then train yourself to respond to what it says. When I did this, I began to hear God speak to me through His Word; eventually, He would speak to me and guide me every day. Most of the time, the Holy Spirit will speak the truth of the Word and give you insight and revelation. Other times, He will be specific and lead you personally. Additionally, angels of the Lord guide you to make sure you meet all your appointments so there are no *disappointments*.

God wants to tell you what will happen in the future. He wants to show you things and knows how much you can and cannot handle. There is a fire from the altar that you need to encounter, which will burn out all the chaff. I have found there is a lot within us that hinders us from hearing God's voice. I believe that right now, the holy fire is baptizing you as you read this. Ask the Lord to baptize you with His holy fire. Let the coal from the altar of God touch your lips and bring change. Being baptized in the holy fire is a powerful experience you can have.

Prayer for Holy Fire

> *Father, I pray right now that You speak to me.*
> *Baptize me in the holy fire that is from the altar.*
> *Begin to burn up anything that is hindering me.*
> *Have Your way with me, Holy Spirit. Burn up*
> *all the chaff and all of the excess baggage that is*
> *not needed. I want to be tried in the fire so only*
> *the purest gold comes out. I submit to the fire*
> *right now, in the name of Jesus.*

GIVING GLORY AND HONOR

You will always have everything that you need when you submit to the holy fire. You will be protected, and the devil will be unable to touch you when you are in it. By the Holy Spirit, I can see there is much provision coming in. Begin to get excited and trust God for the provision that is coming. God has heard all your prayers, and He is going to respond to your needs. Continue to talk to Him as a person. Tell God how much you love Him and trust Him. Tell Him He is beautiful and powerful and He deserves all the glory. Give everything back to Him and do not take any glory for yourself. Bow down and worship Him. Continually acknowledge Him, and He will begin to speak to you!

> *For My thoughts are not your thoughts, nor are your ways My ways," says the Lord. "For as the heavens are higher than the earth, so are My ways higher than your ways, and My thoughts than your thoughts.*
>
> —ISAIAH 55:8-9

We must be careful not to get into the mental realm. I know that is easier said than done, but we must stay out of our own understanding. There are ways about God that we do not understand because God is so mighty and powerful and full of wisdom. God has given us the Holy Spirit, who brings us discernment and revelation.

> *And my speech and my preaching were not with persuasive words of human wisdom, but in*

demonstration of the Spirit and of power, that
your faith should not be in the wisdom of men but
in the power of God.

—1 CORINTHIANS 2:4-5

Paul was a scholar and was even being mentored to become a leader of the Pharisees. Jesus intercepted him on the road to Damascus, and he became an apostle of the Lord. Paul told the Corinthians that he did not come with enticing words of man's wisdom, but rather, he came in power and with the demonstration of the Holy Spirit. He told them that he used to come another way, but from that point forward he trusted in the power of God and in what the Spirit says.

But as it is written: "Eye has not seen, nor ear
heard, nor have entered into the heart of man the
things which God has prepared for those who love
Him." But God has revealed them to us through
His Spirit. For the Spirit searches all things, yes,
the deep things of God. For what man knows the
things of a man except the spirit of the man which
is in him? Even so no one knows the things of God
except the Spirit of God.

—1 CORINTHIANS 2:9-11

The Holy Spirit gives us things from the other realm. You have been born again of the Spirit, and inside of you is a new man. You are a new creature in Christ; old things have passed away (see 2 Corinthians 5:17). Since you have been born of the Spirit, you now have the ability to hear from God; you now know your Father's voice.

My sheep hear My voice, and I know them, and they follow Me.

—JOHN 10:27

Paul is saying that the Spirit wants to reveal the ways and intentions of God. God does want to speak to you, but He will speak to you through your spirit. You must quiet yourself and listen, and you will be able to hear Him in your spirit. He is leading and guiding you. You may only sense His answer as a red or green light; it may even be like "a knowing" as opposed to a feeling.

I have learned to get into a peaceful place, and there I am able to hear the voice of God. Remember that if you hear His voice, you must also have an understanding of His ways. Everything that you hear must match up with the Word of God. There are evil spirits and familiar spirits that will try to speak to you as well. You can combat this by continually meditating on the Word of God and trusting in Him. Quote the Word of God day and night and tell the Lord how much you trust and love Him. Thank Him that He is making His voice clear to you and that His ways and His will are being revealed to you.

When you do this, the Holy Spirit will fortify you, and you will begin to see your world change. A flip happened in my life when I realized I was not a victim anymore and that God had delivered me and given me favor. At that point, I began working in synchronization with Heaven. I wanted the fullness of what had been written about me in Heaven. I began telling God how much I love Him and how much I wanted to fulfill His plan for me. I would tell Him that I believe that the angels are leading and guiding me and the Holy Spirit is opening the realms of wisdom and the treasuries of understanding. As I spoke that every day and repeated Scriptures about wisdom, I began to hear the voice of God. I started to feel like I was being led all the time. I recognize the still small voice of the Lord.

As sons and daughters, God wants to whisper to us. He wants us to understand His intentions and His will for our lives. I was also reminded that God could speak very loudly and He could present Himself as the God described in Psalm 29. But He wants to lovingly whisper to you, and if His Word is not in your heart, it will limit you from hearing His voice.

When I was in Heaven, I realized that what God wanted to speak to me was too good for me to handle. When I came back, I was able to expect good things to happen. I can expect demons to get out of my way, and I can expect His supernatural provision. I can expect to reach as many people as possible with the gospel. I know all of this to be true because I know that the angels of the Lord, the Holy Spirit, and the Father are working with me. Because of this, I know the only real hindrance to me is if I let the devil hinder me, oppose myself, or disagree with God's will.

If you find that you are opposing God's Word, or His will for you, you must get rid of rebellion and any thoughts that are against what God has already revealed.

> *For though we walk in the flesh, we do not war according to the flesh. For the weapons of our war-fare are not carnal but mighty in God for pulling down strongholds, casting down arguments and*

every high thing that exalts itself against the knowledge of God, bringing every thought into captivity to the obedience of Christ, and being ready to punish all disobedience when your obedience is fulfilled.

—2 CORINTHIANS 10:3-6

In this Scripture, Paul says that we must "take every thought captive." We can see that this happens in the mental realm. We need to make sure that all of our thoughts are obedient to the Word. God will speak truth to our hearts. But our minds have strongholds, and we must pull them down. We must know that God loves us, and there is no condemnation for those who are in Christ Jesus (see Romans 8:1). We cannot let fear torment our thoughts, for perfect love drives out fear (1 John 4:18).

When you do not know what to do in a situation, God is faithful. He will lead you; allow Him also to lead you into correction and discipline. When you obey what God says in the Word, you frame your thinking and align your mindset with the Spirit. Your mind and your spirit then begin to work together. When this happens, the Lord will begin to speak to you in a mighty way.

It is vital that you deal with the demonic forces around you by discerning the voices and discerning what is right and wrong. You must measure everything by the Word of God and by the witness of the Spirit. I use Ephesians 1:17-23 as a prayer and continually ask God for wisdom and discernment, so my eyes are enlightened with His will and way.

That the God of our Lord Jesus Christ, the Father of glory, may give to you the spirit of wisdom and revelation in the knowledge of Him, the eyes of your understanding being enlightened; that you may know what is the hope of His calling, what are the riches of the glory of His inheritance in the saints, and what is the exceeding greatness of His power toward us who believe, according to the working of His mighty power which He worked in Christ when He raised Him from the dead and seated Him at His right hand in the heavenly places, far above all principality and power and might and dominion, and every name that is named, not only in this age but also in that which is to come. And He put all things under His feet, and gave Him to be head over all things to the church, which is His body, the fullness of Him who fills all in all.

—EPHESIANS 1:17-23

As I rehearse these things that Paul said to the Ephesians, I also pray them for myself. When I do, the Spirit of God has the ability to talk to me. He guides me, and we commune together.

Your ability to hear clearly begins with concentrating on Romans 8 and removing condemnation from your life.

There is therefore now no condemnation to those who are in Christ Jesus, who do not walk according to the flesh, but according to the Spirit.

—ROMANS 8:1

We do not war just in our minds, but we fight with our flesh that tries to act up. We engage in warfare by practicing what we have heard. In 1 Timothy 1:18, Paul tells Timothy to use the prophecies that he had received in order to wage good warfare. In other words, we can wage war by speaking out prophetic words. Proclaim and reinforce God's Word as a form of warfare; the Spirit realm will respond to our voices.

Once I began to speak out and prophesy from what was in my spirit, repeating the Word of God and praying in the Spirit, I found that I could speak to my mountains and they started being removed! The Lord would give me affirmation. He would speak to me and visit me; I saw this turn for me. This will happen for you also, but you must understand the importance of spiritual warfare. You must be disciplined to initiate warfare in the spirit by the fire of God, and you must bring down the strongholds in your mind and correct your thoughts. Your mindset should reflect the intentions of God.

When you come against evil spirits, you come against the enemies of God. They are God's enemies and your enemies, and they are working against God. Jesus went around healing everyone who was oppressed of the devil, and that is what you are supposed to be doing as well. You are to be doing good and healing everyone oppressed of the devil. This is what God is doing on the earth right now through Christians.

When you pray, your prayer should be, "Thy kingdom come Thy will be done on the earth as it is in Heaven." As a son or a daughter, you are asking your Father to bring His will and His ways into the earth. You are asking for His intentions to come into the earth through you. This is what Isaiah did when he encountered the throne room. He saw that his lips needed to be cleansed, so the coal from the altar was given to him by an angel. Once the coal touched him, then he needed to go back and tell the people (see Isaiah 6).

This is happening with you right now! You are being sent out as an ambassador. From now on, your whole life will be very powerful because you are hearing the voice of the Lord and focusing on your place in Heaven. It is changing you. You believe in Jesus Christ, and you have been washed in the blood. You must repent of your sins and daily turn back to Jesus so that you are always keeping everything clear and clean before Him. You are sealed in the Lamb's Book of Life.

If we daily confess our sins and areas where we fall short, God is faithful to forgive us.

> *If we confess our sins, He is faithful and just to forgive us our sins and to cleanse us from all unrighteousness.*
>
> —1 John 1:9

We are supposed to walk in this fellowship with Him, keeping ourselves clear. Many people are hindered by their guilty consciences. This Scripture verse tells us that when we confess our sins, He cleanses us from all unrighteousness. This verse is not for unbelievers but it is for Christians.

God is with you in a mighty way, and He is speaking to you. Begin to focus on His voice inside of you and come against any familiar spirit and anything that exalts itself above the knowledge of God. We must learn to handcuff anything to the contrary and bring it into captivity.

Breakthrough Prayer

> *I break all hindrances over you. Lord, I thank You for the fire going through them right now. Lord, I thank You that You are giving them the confidence to speak to their mountains and to speak out what You are speaking over them. They will not only hear Your voice, but they will listen and obey. I pray that you will begin to prophesy to your world. Lord, give them the words to speak, and let the devils flee in the name of Jesus. The fire of God is all over you and in your life. God is sending you out as an ambassador, and He is taking off the limitations so you can hear His voice!*

A STORY

I remember hearing the mighty, thundering voice of the Lord one particular time. Usually, He speaks to me in a still small voice, which may be hard to distinguish if you are too busy and distracted. It is rare to hear His voice audibly, but it is very profound when it does happen.

I had just arrived in a new city in 1985 in order to finish up my education with a two-year program after completing my bachelor's degree. I was initially staying with a friend. The two of us had completed our bachelor degrees together at the same college a year prior.

I remember that as I awakened one morning, my room was full of the glory of the Lord. The atmosphere was pure and holy as I heard the audible voice of God speak to me from a cloud in the room. The heavenly Father spoke these words to me: "Kevin, while you are in this city nothing shall be impossible to you!" The voice shook the house, and I heard the very frame of the house vibrate. While I lived in that city for the next three years, nothing was impossible to me! God moved in a supernatural way to confirm His perfect will for me for that, but God speaking audibly is very rare. I will never forget that morning!

Chapter 3

CREATED IN HIS IMAGE

So God created man in His own image; in the image of
God He created him; male and female He created them.

—GENESIS 1:27

ONE OF THE THINGS I SAW WHEN I WAS IN HEAVEN WAS
that the Lord Himself made man in His own image. Man and
woman were created so they could communicate with God.
There is an exclusivity that happens between a human being and
God that no other created beings have. This close affinity with
God enables you to communicate with your Creator in an intimate way. Genesis 1:27 shows that God's original plan for man
was that we would be just like Him. We, of course, are not God,
and we know that. Yet, we are *like* Him because we have been
made in His image.

> *Therefore, if anyone is in Christ, he is a new cre-*
> *ation; old things have passed away; behold, all*
> *things have become new.*
>
> —2 CORINTHIANS 5:17

We use this verse in Second Corinthians because it describes the born-again experience Jesus talked about with Nicodemus. In John 3:3, *"Jesus answered and said to him, 'Most assuredly, I say to you, unless one is born again, he cannot see the Kingdom of God.'"* It is very important for you to understand that you are a spiritual being first, you live in a body, and you have a soul. Your soul is where your mind, will, and emotions are, and this is the way that God created you. When you were born again, God caused your *spirit* to become born again, as the Scripture says, *"Behold, all things have become new."* You are now a new creation in Christ Jesus by the power of the Holy Spirit. In your heart, your inner man, you can now communicate with God one-on-one. In First Corinthians 6:19, Paul says, *"Or do you not know that your body is the temple of the Holy Spirit who is in you, whom you have from God, and you are not your own?"* In First Corinthians 6:17, it states, *"But he who is joined to the Lord is one spirit with Him."* You are created in the image of God, and God has made a way for you, and all Christians, to communicate with Him at all times within your inner man.

YOUR TRANSLATOR: THE HOLY SPIRIT

Unfortunately, many people tell me that they cannot hear God's voice. But consider this. When I travel, I sometimes do not know the language. There is a language barrier, and therefore, there is need of a translator. In Christianity, your translator is the Holy Spirit. You do not have to know the language of the Spirit; you only have to yield to the Holy Spirit, and He prays for you. The Holy Spirit does not do all the work. You have to yield to Him, but He helps you and gives you the words to speak. The Spirit also gives you wisdom and knowledge. Even if you cannot hear God's voice with your physical ears, there is something spiritual happening inside of you all the time in your heart.

In your ways of expressing your faith in Jesus, you do not always know how to pray, and you often do not know how to testify about Jesus. Sometimes you have trouble talking about the Lord to others. The Spirit of God came on the Day of Pentecost to baptize believers in the Holy Spirit with the evidence of speaking in other tongues and power (see Acts 2:1-4). When you have this experience, God gives you the power to pray and the power to testify of Jesus to others. When you accept Jesus Christ into your heart, you also can have the experience of being baptized in the Holy Spirit with the evidence of speaking in other tongues. This baptism of the Holy Spirit is a separate experience that causes you to walk in the power of the Holy Spirit.

> *Behold, I send the Promise of My Father upon you; but tarry in the city of Jerusalem until you are endued with power from on high.*
> —LUKE 24:49

Jesus told believers to wait in the city until they were endued with power from on high. Faith is of the heart, and it is the substance of things hoped for and the evidence of things not seen (see Hebrews 11:1). *"But without faith it is impossible to please Him, for he who comes to God must believe that He is, and that He is a rewarder of those who diligently seek Him"* (Hebrews 11:6). Faith is not a mental endeavor. Faith is of the heart, and it pleases God. Whoever comes to God must believe that He is and believe that God rewards those who diligently seek Him. When you are born again of the Spirit, the power of God comes into your heart. The Holy Spirit is the one who caused you to be born again. The Holy Spirit will never leave you. He is in you, and He causes your spirit to change into what God wants you to be. God wants you to be the righteousness of God in Christ Jesus (see 2 Corinthians 5:21). God wants you to be holy as He is holy (1 Peter 1:16). These requirements are met through the Holy Spirit within you as you yield to the Spirit and not the flesh (Galatians 5:16).

> *I say then: Walk in the Spirit, and you shall not fulfill the lust of the flesh.*
>
> —GALATIANS 5:16

YIELD TO THE SPIRIT: SUBMIT THE FLESH

The Holy Spirit is part of the Trinity—Father, Son, and Holy Spirit. Those three talk to each other, and the Holy Spirit inside of you communicates with the Father and Son and then with your spirit. There is a spiritual communion going on inside of you—and every believer—even right now as you are reading this. The Holy Spirit within you is communicating with you and talking to you. You are a child of God, and when you were born again, you were adopted into God's family (see Ephesians 1:5). You are now separate from the world.

The world has a voice, and God has a voice. But with the Word of God and the Spirit of God, you can hear from God all the time. You have the Word of God written in the Bible so you can read and meditate on it (see Joshua 1:8). You also have the Spirit of God inside you to build you up in your most holy faith praying in the Holy Spirit (see Jude 20). When the Word and the Spirit in you meet, then you have the power to enter heavenly realms and experience spiritual things.

The Holy Bible has been around for a long time and people read the Bible every day, but they do not have spiritual experiences. Then there are people who have the Spirit of God, but they do not have the Word of God. They are not grounded in the Word, and yet, they have all kinds of spiritual experiences. I have noticed that people like this get off track doctrinally because they are not in the Word of God as well. When you have the Spirit of God *and* the Word of God, then you have a tremendous amount of power made available to you.

Jesus died on the cross to redeem you back to the Father. He did not redeem your flesh or your mind but your spirit. Your spiritual life is taken care of because it is a spiritual experience. The apostle Paul talked about the three parts of man, your spirit, soul, and body. Your spirit must be born again, but your soul— or your mind, will, and emotions—must be transformed by the God's Word and Spirit. Your body is another entity entirely. I call your body your earth suit because you must have one to live on the earth. What your body needs is discipline and control.

Paul said it this way, "...*I discipline my body and bring it into subjection, lest, when I have preached to others, I myself should become disqualified*" (1 Corinthians 9:27). We are not supposed to yield to the flesh but to the Spirit, and those do yield to the Spirit of God are sons of God.

> *For if you live according to the flesh you will die;*
> *but if by the Spirit you put to death the deeds of*
> *the body, you will live. For as many as are led by*
> *the Spirit of God, these are sons of God.*
> —ROMANS 8:13-14

HIS PLAN FOR RELATIONSHIP

Revisiting the idea of being created in the image of God, the following verses are important for you to meditate on. As you grasp what God did for man in the beginning, you will see where you now stand through your born-again experience and the baptism of the Holy Spirit. You will understand why you have the Word of God and the Spirit of God. You will see how all these promises help you in this fallen world where you are redeemed but the world is not. Jesus died for every single person. He made the way so every single person who walks this earth can repent, stop sinning, turn to the Lord Jesus Christ, be redeemed, walk with God, and go to Heaven.

> *Then God said, "Let Us make man in Our image,*
> *according to Our likeness; let them have domin-*
> *ion over the fish of the sea, over the birds of the*
> *air, and over the cattle, over all the earth and over*

every creeping thing that creeps on the earth." So
God created man in His own image; in the image
of God He created him; male and female He cre-
ated them. Then God blessed them, and God said
to them, "Be fruitful and multiply; fill the earth
and subdue it; have dominion over the fish of the
sea, over the birds of the air, and over every living
thing that moves on the earth."

—Genesis 1:26-28

When God says, "Let *us* make man in our image," He uses the plural word *us* referring to the Trinity. It's always been God's intent for the holy Trinity and man to communicate. God's original intent from the very beginning was for you to have a relationship with Him that was intimate. He wants you to hear His voice, and He wants to hear yours. It is not always your fault that you cannot hear God's voice, but it is because you live in a fallen world. That's why you must learn how to operate in this fallen world and in the spirit realm. The spirit realm is perfect and allows you to change and overcome in this natural realm.

God came to Adam and Eve in the cool of the day to walk and talk with them in the garden (see Genesis 3:8). He wanted to enjoy their fellowship. When Lucifer saw this, he was very jealous. In fact, I believe jealousy filled him to such a point that he caused man to fall as a result. After Adam and Eve sinned, they were sent away from the garden, and they no longer enjoyed the intimate relationship with God they once had. We now suffer their same fate when we are born into this fallen world. We do not know anything about our Creator or this life because man is lost. That is why God came through Jesus Christ to redeem us back to Himself. God never intended man to do some of the things that he does on this earth. There is no way that God created man to kill each other or do the vile things happening in the world today. Second Peter 1:4 tells us what Jesus Christ came to do for us. He came to give us great promises and the fulfillment of Scripture. The fulfillment of the mystery of the ages was that God would buy back man and restore him back in relationship and fellowship with God our Creator.

> *By which have been given to us exceedingly great*
> *and precious promises, that through these you may*
> *be partakers of the divine nature, having escaped*
> *the corruption that is in the world through lust.*
> —2 PETER 1:4

RESTORED WITH AUTHORITY

God has given us powerful and precious promises, and when we partake of these benefits of God, we partake of His divine nature. In other words, we can actually partake of God's spiritual nature. Peter wrote about this because he understood that Jesus Christ came to restore us spiritually, not physically. Many of the disciples were disappointed when they found out that Jesus did not come to set Himself up as King and drive Rome out of Israel. But Jesus came with an even higher purpose—to buy back humanity. That plan unfolded later on as we read in Peter's epistles.

Think about it. *You* are a partaker of the divine nature, and authority has been given to you as well. Part of that divine nature is kingship or ambassadorship, which means you are an authority figure in the Kingdom of God.

> *Behold, I give you the authority to trample on serpents and scorpions, and over all the power of the enemy, and nothing shall by any means hurt you.*
> —LUKE 10:19

Jesus restored you back with God by giving you authority just like Adam had in the garden. God gave Adam dominion over the fish of the sea, the birds of the air, all the animals, and everything on the earth. Jesus Christ, through the born-again experience, has redeemed you, and you can experience deliverance not only in your own life but in the body of Christ. There are many people who need deliverance from the demonic, and God has given us this authority through Jesus Christ. Jesus said to use His name to drive out devils. When you administer authority, you are essentially enforcing what Jesus did on the cross and the demons know that. They know who you represent when you use the name of Jesus; His name and His blood are very powerful. The Spirit of God comes upon you and ignites your inner man and then starts to reveal to you some of the benefits you have in Christ Jesus. You have been restored back in your spirit to the things of God that He had for you before man fell.

GOD DESIRES TO SPEAK TO YOU

To fulfill all righteousness while He was on earth, Jesus Himself submitted to being baptized in water just as you do when you are baptized in water. When Jesus was baptized, the Holy Spirit came upon Him, and the voice of the Father from Heaven spoke. God said, *"This is My beloved Son, in whom I am well pleased"* (see Matthew 3). That is exactly how the Father feels about you. You are His child, a son or daughter of a loving God, and because of that you can hear the Father speak to you just like He spoke to Jesus. You now have the same relationship with the Father because you are a co-heir with Christ and an heir of God as His child (see Romans 8:17). There are more dimensions in the spiritual realm than you can imagine.

Picture Jesus' baptism with me. Imagine Jesus in the water. He is part of the Trinity, and the Holy Spirit descends like a dove upon Jesus, another part of the Trinity. The Father, another part of the Trinity, speaks in an audible voice from Heaven. All three persons in one—the Holy Trinity—take part in the moment. Believe that the Father wants to communicate with you even more than you do, and He has set it up so that you can.

> *Then Jesus came from Galilee to John at the Jordan to be baptized by him. And John tried to prevent Him, saying, "I need to be baptized by You, and are You coming to me?" But Jesus answered and said to him, "Permit it to be so now, for thus it is fitting for us to fulfill all righteousness." Then he allowed Him. When He had been baptized, Jesus came up immediately from the water; and behold, the heavens were opened to Him, and He saw the Spirit of God descending like a dove and alighting upon Him. And*

suddenly a voice came from heaven, saying, "This
is My beloved Son, in whom I am well pleased."
—MATTHEW 3:13-17

Jesus, the Lamb of God, was slain from the foundation of the world; Jesus was pre-existing. *"All who dwell on the earth will worship Him, whose names have not been written in the Book of Life of the Lamb slain from the foundation of the world"* (Revelation 13:8). Jesus is the pre-existing One with the Father. As Jesus prayed to the Father before He left earth, He said, *"And now, O Father, glorify Me together with Yourself, with the glory which I had with You before the world was"* (John 17:5). Jesus was saying that He was with the Father before the world began, and He was about to go back to the glory that He had with the Father.

> *I do not pray for these alone, but also for those who will believe in Me through their word; that they all may be one, as You, Father, are in Me, and I in You; that they also may be one in Us, that the world may believe that You sent Me. And the glory which You gave Me I have given them, that they may be one just as We are one: I in them, and You in Me; that they may be made perfect in one, and that the world may know that You have sent Me, and have loved them as You have loved Me.*
> —JOHN 17:20-23

Just before Jesus was crucified, He prayed to the Father for the disciples, and for all those who would believe in Him, that the Father would make us all one. Jesus prayed that as the

Father and Jesus were one, and in each other, that we would be in them also. This is the level of communication that Jesus had with the Father, and this is what the Father and Jesus want for you. The same relationship that Jesus has with the Father has been given to you.

> *Remember the former things of old, for I am God, and there is no other; I am God, and there is none like Me, declaring the end from the beginning, and from ancient times things that are not yet done saying, "My counsel shall stand, and I will do all My pleasure."*
>
> —ISAIAH 46:9-10

This verse in Isaiah speaks about the pre-existent state of God. Before the worlds were formed, God knew the beginning and the end. God established all things. He is saying that His counsel will stand, and He will do His pleasure. Part of God's pleasure was for you to be restored back to Him with all mankind. Just being a Christian and going to Heaven would be enough, but God kept you on the earth. When you became saved, you were not just raptured right then and there and taken to Heaven.

You are still alive on the earth today, and you still have to go to work. You still have to pay your bills and your taxes. Everything is just like it was except spiritually you now have a relationship with the Father. When you continue to have that relationship, you will see the Kingdom of God start to work out from inside of you. As it begins to work, angels begin to come and help you, and you will start to see blessings in your life and favor. Jesus will start to work His great and mighty power in your life. Your life is all good news, and it is why God came back through Jesus Christ.

> *Your eyes saw my substance, being yet unformed.*
> *And in Your book they all were written, the days*
> *fashioned for me, when as yet there were none of*
> *them.*
>
> —PSALM 139:16

God wrote a book about you in Heaven before you were ever born. Each one of your days were written before even one of them came to pass. God saw your body being formed in your mother's womb (see Psalm 139). God loves you and will never leave you an orphan. God has a plan for your life, and you have nothing to worry about.

A STORY

I recall the time when the Lord started to teach me to speak to the mountains in my life. Jesus had revealed to me that humans had originally been created in the image of God, according to Genesis 1:26. When Jesus taught concerning speaking to mountains in Mark 11:23-24, He was addressing the fact that believers are born-again, spirit beings made in the image of God. From this condition, we are to speak like God speaks and see our roadblocks removed.

When I was in college, I needed a vehicle to get to school and work. I remember praying in the Spirit and knowing what particular car and price I was to believe for. I immediately felt to call my dad, who was unsaved at the time. I told him that I was believing for a used blue Datsun car for $1500. When I said it this to him, I felt the power of God as I repeated what the Spirit of God had spoken to me. Later, a friend called and told me of a car that he found in the local paper for sale. I called the number and bought the car. It was the exact car and price I had spoken. When my dad heard this, he began to believe in the Lord because of the manifestation of my faith before his very eyes.

Chapter 4

YOU HAVE BEEN PREDESTINED

And now, O Father, glorify Me together with Yourself, with the glory which I had with You before the world was.

—JOHN 17:5

THE WHOLE IDEA OF PREDESTINATION IS THAT JESUS Christ Himself sat with the Father and with the Holy Spirit in eternity before man was ever formed. Together, the Holy Trinity thought and discussed what they were going to do with creation, and then decided to make man in their image. From that point onward, everything that was created—the earth and everything in it—God made especially for man. God was already complete and had everything He needed in Heaven. When God lost man in the garden, He already had planned for a way of redemption through Jesus Christ. Jesus was the Lamb of God that was slain from the foundation of the world (see Revelation 13:8).

> *But I make known to you, brethren, that the gospel which was preached by me is not according to man. For I neither received it from man, nor was I taught it, but it came through the revelation of Jesus Christ. For you have heard of my former conduct in Judaism, how I persecuted the church of God beyond measure and tried to destroy it. And I advanced in Judaism beyond many of my contemporaries in my own nation, being more exceedingly zealous for the traditions of my fathers. But when it pleased God, who separated me from my mother's womb and called me through His grace, to reveal His Son in me, that I might preach Him among the Gentiles, I did not immediately confer with flesh and blood, nor did I go up to Jerusalem to those who were apostles before me; but I went to Arabia, and returned again to Damascus.*
>
> —GALATIANS 1:11-17

Here in Galatians, Paul is talking about the earthly plan that he and the Jewish leaders had for his life. There were plans made for Paul to excel and become the leader of the Pharisees. Paul was being groomed and called himself a "Pharisee of the Pharisees." It was revealed to Paul that God had separated him from his mother's womb to be an apostle and to preach Christ to the Gentiles. God's plan for his life was so contrary to the plans of man for his life. Paul had a supernatural conversion and calling from God (see Acts 9:1-42). God had already destined Paul to be an apostle on the earth, and it had nothing to do with the plans of man for his life.

THE MYSTERY OF HIS WILL

It is the same with you! God will speak into your life and cause you to do what He wants you to do, but it has to be by revelation. Paul did not confer with any man about God's plan for his life because God had destined this before he was ever born. Before Paul's supernatural call from God, he had rejected Jesus and was persecuting Christians. Later, however, Paul found himself preaching Jesus to the unclean people, the Gentiles, and this was the perfect will of God for his life. Paul said that he was predestined, set apart from birth, to be an apostle and preach the gospel of Jesus Christ to the Gentiles. According to the Jewish people, the Gentiles were not redeemable, and they were considered unclean because they were not part of God's people.

> *Blessed be the God and Father of our Lord Jesus Christ, who has blessed us with every spiritual blessing in the heavenly places in Christ, just as He chose us in Him before the foundation of the world, that we should be holy and without blame before Him in love, having predestined us to adoption as sons by Jesus Christ to Himself, according to the good pleasure of His will, to the praise of the glory of His grace, by which He made us accepted in the Beloved. In Him we have redemption*

*through His blood, the forgiveness of sins, accord-
ing to the riches of His grace which He made to
abound toward us in all wisdom and prudence,
having made known to us the mystery of His will,
according to His good pleasure which He purposed
in Himself, that in the dispensation of the fullness
of the times He might gather together in one all
things in Christ, both which are in heaven and
which are on earth—in Him. In Him also we
have obtained an inheritance, being predestined
according to the purpose of Him who works all
things according to the counsel of His will, that we
who first trusted in Christ should be to the praise
of His glory.*

—EPHESIANS 1:3-12

In these verses, Paul is explaining what happened to him and God's plan for you and all of mankind. Paul is telling you that God has already blessed you with every spiritual blessing in the heavenly places in Christ Jesus. Christ chose you before the foundation of the world and loved you before you were even born. Even though God knew that man would fall, He had already planned everything out and prepared the way for salvation. Paul says that you are holy and without blame before God in love. You accept the fact that God took the blame away from you—and He did it before you were ever born. For those who do not accept what Jesus did for them and do not acknowledge Him, they will eventually die in their sins. That would mean they will go to hell for their sins.

You have already been adopted-in by Jesus because of what He did for you on the cross. He died in your place, and now because of sonship, you can know the mystery of His will. It can be revealed to you! At any one moment, the Holy Spirit can breathe on you and show you the truth in the Word of God. Revelation is part of God's predestined plan for you, and everything you are to receive through Jesus Christ was already planned before Jesus ever came unto the earth in the flesh.

When you give yourself over to God and bend your will to Him, you will begin to realize that you are in the family of God. You will start to live and move and have your being in Him (see Acts 17:28). The purpose of God for your life will start working in you. It is the will of God in Heaven for you that you will start to see on the earth. That is what happened with Paul. He realized that Jesus Christ was the One who had written a book about him in Heaven before he was ever born (see Psalm 139:16).

GIVE YOURSELF OVER TO GOD

As he journeyed he came near Damascus, and suddenly a light shone around him from heaven. Then he fell to the ground, and heard a voice saying to him, "Saul, Saul, why are you persecuting Me?" And he said, "Who are You, Lord?" Then the Lord said, "I am Jesus, whom you are persecuting. It is hard for you to kick against the goads." So he, trembling and astonished, said, "Lord, what do You want me to do?" Then the

Lord said to him, "Arise and go into the city, and
you will be told what you must do."

—ACTS 9:3-6

When Paul met Jesus on the road to Damascus, Jesus asked him why he was persecuting Him. It was then that Paul realized that the Christians he was killing and persecuting were part of the inheritance of God. Paul was arrested by God and blinded. He found himself vulnerable and at God's mercy. When Jesus told Paul that he was kicking against the goads, Paul realized that he had been working against the purposes of God in his life. Realizing that we are working against God and His will happens to all of us as Christians. However, when you become born again and bend your will to His, you will have a direct line of communication open to Him. From that point forward, the Spirit of God is in your spirit inside you, and the Holy Spirit and your spirit talk with each other. The Holy Spirit, as a part of the Holy Trinity (the Father, Son, and Holy Spirit), and your spirit are *all* communicating. You can participate in the fullness of what Jesus Christ bought for you, and you can hear His voice. This is one of the benefits you receive when you are born again.

But even if our gospel is veiled, it is veiled to those
who are perishing, whose minds the god of this age
has blinded, who do not believe, lest the light of
the gospel of the glory of Christ, who is the image
of God, should shine on them.

—2 CORINTHIANS 4:3-4

Paul makes it very clear in this verse, in Second Corinthians, that the god of this world has blinded people, so that they do not believe. When the light of the gospel comes in and you are shown the glory of Jesus Christ, then your eyes are opened and then you repent. God does just what He did with Paul. He has to show up and reveal Himself, so you are healed from your spiritual blindness. The god of this world is Satan, and he has blinded the minds of those who do not believe from seeing the glorious light of the good news.

Jesus Christ is the exact image of the Father, and you were created in His image according to the likeness of God. When you receive Jesus, you receive the Holy Spirit, and the Holy Spirit will lead you to the Father. The Holy Spirit will help you to communicate with the Father in your spirit. Even though Jesus came in the flesh to earth, He existed with the Father before the world began. Jesus is the image of the Father in the flesh.

You were spiritually made like God to communicate with God, but your flesh has fallen. Your flesh does not communicate with God, and neither does your mind. Jesus walked as Emmanuel (God with us) on this earth, and He showed us how to operate in two realms. Jesus was the Master of both realms, and He could walk in the Spirit and walk in the flesh. He was God with us. *"And the Word became flesh and dwelt among us, and we beheld His glory, the glory as of the only begotten of the Father, full of grace and truth"* (John 1:14). Jesus took on a body and lived His life on this earth successfully showing us how to walk in the supernatural lifestyle every day. When Jesus handed Himself over and was crucified, it was for our redemption.

> *Beloved, now we are children of God; and it has not yet been revealed what we shall be, but we*

know that when He is revealed, we shall be like
Him, for we shall see Him as He is. And everyone
who has this hope in Him purifies himself, just as
He is pure.

—1 JOHN 3:2-3

You do look like Jesus! When He appears, you will see Him as He is, and you will see that you are like Him. It is very important to realize that while you are here, you are in the image of God. *"Therefore be imitators of God as dear children. And walk in love, as Christ also has loved us and given Himself for us, an offering and a sacrifice to God for a sweet-smelling aroma"* (Ephesians 5:1-2). Here Paul is encouraging you to imitate God in the way you talk and walk. This is what children do; they imitate their parents. You imitate your Father God, and you imitate Jesus and how He walked on this earth. You are a good child, growing up just like your Father, which is what Jesus and the Holy Spirit were sent to help you do. You want to grow up and be mature, and that is something that the apostle Paul talked about all the time. We have been restored back to what Adam was before the fall, and that is what the gospel did spiritually for us.

Twice Moses spent forty days on Mount Sinai with God. His face actually became transformed to the point where beams of light were coming out of his face because he had been face to face with God for so many days. The Israelites were afraid to look at Moses when he came down from the mountain because his face shown, and Moses had to wear a veil over his face (see Exodus 34:29-35). Moses probably did not even know how long he was up on the mountain with God; to him it may have felt as though no time had passed. When you are with God, there is no time; it is suspended, and Moses probably did not age a bit during those days with God. His face was restored back to what Adam was before the fall, and because of that, he was fearful looking to the people. Remember, God made you in His image. Moses likely experienced the glory realm, and even his flesh conformed to the pure plan of God from the beginning just by his association with God.

> *For He has not put the world to come, of which we speak, in subjection to angels. But one testified in a certain place, saying: "What is man that You are mindful of him, or the son of man that You take care of him? You have made him a little lower than the angels; You have crowned him with glory and honor, and set him over the works of Your hands. You have put all things in subjection under his feet." For in that He put all in subjection under him, He left nothing that is not put under him. But now we do not yet see all things put under him. But we see Jesus, who was made a little lower than the angels, for the suffering of death crowned with glory and honor, that He, by the grace of God, might taste death for everyone.*
>
> —HEBREWS 2:5-9

Jesus was made lower than the angels, became flesh, and walked perfectly on earth; then He took upon Himself the sin in your life. Jesus took your place on the cross, and everything is now under Jesus' feet. And if it's under His feet, it's under our feet as the Church. The church is the body of Christ, and Jesus is the head. The body of Christ has dominion because Jesus has given us everything. When you know who you are in Christ and you use your God-given authority, demons know this. The demons think that Jesus is talking to them because you represent Him. You are an ambassador of Jesus Christ and the Kingdom of Heaven. Jesus is your focus until everything comes into alignment in the millennial reign (see Revelation 20:4-6). One day you will rule and reign with Jesus in the millennial reign because everything has been put under Him. For now, we still live in a fallen world where terrible things happen because the god of this world is still here. But, praise God, you and I can take authority over the devil and his demons in Jesus' name.

Paul was caught up to Heaven and saw that his name was already written in the Lamb's Book of Life, he was going to be an apostle, and he would preach to the Gentiles. God knows everything. In fact, He already knows the decisions that you are yet to make in your life. God did not make Paul repent, and He did not make Paul become an apostle, but these were things God knew ahead of time. Because of that, God had to wait for Paul to come to the end of himself. The biblical way to view predestination is that God already knows the end from the beginning. God understands that your will is your own, and He won't *make* you do anything. Yet that does not stop God from writing a wonderful plan for each human being on the earth. But you can override God's plan with your will and do what you want to do. Sadly, there are people in hell right now because they died in sin and rebellion and did not repent of their sins. They were cast into hell even though their books in Heaven reflected the wonderful things that God had planned for them.

The concept of predestination is that God knows ahead of time what decisions you will make, but He does not manipulate you to make them. He just writes a book about you. He created you with a plan for your life, and God acts as though you are coming to Heaven. It is up to every individual to receive that plan or to reject it because of his or her own will. People do not understand that their own wills can be a great asset or a great liability. Your will can sometimes take you to places you should not go. That is why you need to repent daily, turn toward God and walk with Him. Bend your will toward God's will, and in every matter, be humble before Him.

Paul had to get knocked off of his horse on the road to Damascus because he was resisting God in rebellion. You do not have to wait to find God that way. You can just accept the plan of God for your life now. You can accept what Jesus has done on the cross for you and then allow God's voice to start speaking to you. When you are born again, you can listen to the still small voice inside of you and receive guidance and direction from Heaven. Listen and obey to the voice of God so you don't find yourself resisting and rebelling against Him. Every Christian has the ability to hear the voice of God. God loves you, and He has written a wonderful book about you in Heaven (see Psalm 139:16).

GOD OUTSIDE OF TIME

You've gone into my future to prepare the way,
and in kindness you follow behind me to spare me
from the harm of my past. With your hand of love
upon my life, you impart a blessing to me.
—PSALM 139:5 TPT

God has even gone into your future and made a path for you. He is standing in your future waiting on you. God also goes behind you to protect you from the harm and hurt of your past. God is all around you, and He has written these wonderful things about you. An important part of God's plan for you is that you would come to the full knowledge of Him and have an intimate relationship with Him through Jesus. By the power of the Holy Spirit, you would be able to hear the voice of God loud and clear inside your spirit. Before you were ever born this is what God's plan was for you. You have been predestined to walk in the power and destiny of God that was written long ago in Heaven.

A STORY

I remember the first time I visited my friend, Sid Roth, at his studios in Charlotte, North Carolina. We had spoken on the phone several times, but I never had a face-to-face conversation with him. I was shocked when I started to walk through the facilities and realized that I actually had been there several weeks before. I knew where to go and the location of particular offices within the large facility. When I met Sid, it was as if I had known him all my life. Then, I realized that I had been there with him at his facilities, in the spirit, in a dream one night.

If that wasn't enough, I began to know what was going to happen next and in the distant future. We experienced one of the best weeks filming there and that particular show is still one of the most viewed shows in the history of Sid's program.

God can speak to you and may even take you in a dream to your future. You will be in awe as you watch that dream unfold before your very eyes, in the natural realm.

Chapter 5

DOMINION AND AUTHORITY

Then God blessed them, and God said to them, "Be fruitful and multiply; fill the earth and subdue it; have dominion over the fish of the sea, over the birds of the air, and over every living thing that moves on the earth."
—GENESIS 1:28

GOD SITS ON A THRONE AND IS A VERY POWERFUL BEING who dwells in eternity, but He also dwells in those who are humble and contrite in spirit. *"For thus says the High and Lofty One who inhabits eternity, whose name is Holy: 'I dwell in the high and holy place, with him who has a contrite and humble spirit, to revive the spirit of the humble, and to revive the heart of the contrite ones'"* (Isaiah 57:15). God blessed man and woman when He made them and commanded them to be fruitful and multiply. God told them to fill the earth and subdue it and have dominion over the fish of the sea, the birds of the air, and everything that moves on the earth. He told Adam and Even to rule and reign over God's creation. God's intention for man from the beginning was for him to be the head of everything on the earth.

> *I call heaven and earth as witnesses today against you, that I have set before you life and death, blessing and cursing; therefore choose life, that both you and your descendants may live; that you may love the Lord your God, that you may obey His voice, and that you may cling to Him, for He is your life and the length of your days; and that you may dwell in the land which the Lord swore to your fathers, to Abraham, Isaac, and Jacob, to give them.*
>
> —DEUTERONOMY 30:19-20

When Moses took the children of Israel out of Egypt, he told them that they had a choice to make. They could choose to live in the blessings of God or live in the curses of their own ways. They could choose to be the head or the tail (see Deuteronomy 28). Moses urged the people to choose life that they might love the Lord their God and obey His voice that they and their descendants might live. After receiving the laws of God, Moses saw the importance of being obedient to God's ways, His rules, and His laws. Moses saw that by their obedience, the Israelites could walk in God's authority. This concept was part of the restoration of Adam; however, it was through the *law,* which was temporary. Today, through Jesus Christ, we have a new covenant through faith in Jesus' death and resurrection and through faith in what God has spoken. We are ruling and reigning as kings in this life through Christ Jesus.

God has put inside every man the desire to rule and reign and be the head. Every man senses in his heart that he should not be ruled over by others and be a victim. That is why throughout history, there have been rebellions. In Jesus' time, the Romans ruled over the Israelites, who wanted God to deliver them from Rome. Many at that time thought that Jesus had come as the King of the Jews to deliver them from Rome. Jesus, however, had come back for a much higher purpose—to die for the sins of all mankind and redeem us back to the Father.

God always wanted to be the King of Israel, His chosen people. It was never His perfect will for Israel to have any other king. Within man is a desire to conquer and rule over everything and for everything to be in submission to him. However, on the earth today you see people largely in survival mode. When man fell in the garden and was cast out, all creation fell as well. The earth deteriorated, and now things are the opposite of what they should be.

GREATER THAN JOHN THE BAPTIST

Assuredly, I say to you, among those born of women there has not risen one greater than John the Baptist; but he who is least in the kingdom of heaven is greater than he. And from the days of John the Baptist until now the kingdom of heaven suffers violence, and the violent take it by force. For all the prophets and the law prophesied until

*John. And if you are willing to receive it, he is
Elijah who is to come. He who has ears to hear,
let him hear!*

—MATTHEW 11:11-15

Jesus was saying in Matthew 11 that up to a certain point, violent people were taking the kingdom by force. In the Old Testament, the Kingdom of God advanced, and many wars were documented. King David went against different types of people and civilizations that were against the Lord God Almighty. The Kingdom of God on earth advanced at an alarming rate through God's mighty warriors. In the New Testament, Jesus pointed to John the Baptist and said there had not been one greater than John up to that point. That is surprising because John's ministry was peaceful in comparison to what had been accomplished before him. John simply preached repentance and baptized people in the Jordan River, and yet, Jesus said he was the greatest. In other words, the Kingdom of God in the New Testament was advancing *spiritually* without the violence seen in the Old Testament.

Jesus went on to say that anyone who is least in the Kingdom of God is *greater* than John the Baptist. The body of Christ was formed on the day of Pentecost when the Holy Spirit came. Pentecost happened after John the Baptist was beheaded, and Jesus had ascended to the Father. The Holy Spirit came to baptize people with the evidence of speaking in tongues. Pentecost enabled the born-again believer to receive the Holy Spirit within them. The Kingdom of God is now within you when you accept Jesus Christ as Lord, and you are baptized in the Holy Spirit.

Now you can hear the voice of God because the Kingdom of God and God's supernatural world is right inside of you.

Let me stop here and tell you what I saw when I was sent back from the dead. I was in the operating room standing beside my body, and Jesus was talking to me. Then Jesus took me and showed me many amazing things. It took me a long time to digest everything I heard and saw while I was with Him. One thing I saw was that all of us in the Kingdom of God from John the Baptist until right now are greater than John. You are greater than all the people in the Old Testament, which does not seem right because you think of Moses, Elijah, Elisha, Enoch, Abraham, and all those great people. Jesus said that John was the greatest in the Kingdom until His time.

Yet Jesus said that everyone—even the least of us—is greater than John. John had gone on to be with the Lord before the day of Pentecost, and it is because of Pentecost that the sons of God are revealed in these last days. The children of God are now revealed, and the power of God rests in you and on you through the baptism of the Holy Spirit.

God wants you to speak His Word from the kingdom inside of you where the Holy Spirit dwells. Signs and wonders will follow the speaking and the preaching of the Word of God (see Mark 16:20). Meditate on this profound truth! God wants you to accept the outpouring of the Holy Spirit and the evidence of speaking in tongues. The Spirit of God wants to work through you and show the glory of God through your life and advance the Kingdom of God.

Everyone in the Bible built a foundation for John the Baptist to come, and then John prepared the way for Jesus to come. But just before Jesus ascended to Heaven, He said He was to send the Comforter or the Holy Spirit to the body of Christ. Jesus said that the Church—you and me—would do the works that He did and even greater works than He did because of the Holy Spirit (see John 14:12).

You are supposed to be doing greater works in Jesus because He is continuing to advance the kingdom through you. As a born-again child of God, you are greatest in the Kingdom of God right now. You are at the end of the age, and you have the supernatural power of God within you.

> *He who believes and is baptized will be saved; but he who does not believe will be condemned. And these signs will follow those who believe: In My name they will cast out demons; they will speak with new tongues; they will take up serpents; and if they drink anything deadly, it will by no means hurt them; they will lay hands on the sick, and they will recover.*
>
> —MARK 16:16-18

In these verses, Jesus is telling us that as believers we now have the Kingdom of God inside us. If we believe, signs and wonders will follow us. You will drive out demons—uproot demons from their strongholds and push them out. You will speak in new tongues, which is a supernatural language that did not exist before. You might not know this language, but you will speak as the Spirit gives you utterance. This Scripture also says you will take up serpents or come against anything that tries to harm you. If you drink anything deadly, it will not hurt you. And you will lay hands on the sick, and they will recover. You will have supernatural protection and the miracle of walking in the power and ministry of Jesus Christ.

John the Baptist had no recorded miracles, and yet he was the greatest in the kingdom until that point. He just had one message, and that was a message of repentance. Now, through the revelation of all the sixty-six books in the Bible, you have a gospel you can preach from Genesis to Revelation. You have the full account of what God did for man. You can now preach from every one of those books in the Bible by God's revelation. You can preach the gospel from the Old to the New Testament, and you will have signs following you. That is God's plan for man, and you have been chosen at the end of this age to fulfill His purposes.

When I was in Heaven, I saw that everybody up there wants to meet us because we're the ones chosen at the end of the age to wrap it all up. They think of us as the cream of the crop! Remember, Jesus Christ is God's plan for man from creation until now. He's always been God's plan for man. Jesus Christ is the center of salvation, the Lamb of God slain from the foundations of the world. But God has also chosen you, and you are a part of His plan. I pray that you are hearing God's voice speak to your spirit—bearing witness that you are chosen to display the works of Jesus. Trust that still small voice inside you. Do you see how wonderful it is to hear and discern God's voice?

THE COVENANT REESTABLISHED

So God blessed Noah and his sons, and said to them: "Be fruitful and multiply, and fill the earth. And the fear of you and the dread of you shall be on every beast of the earth, on every bird of the air, on all that move on the earth, and on all the fish of the sea. They are given into your hand. Every moving thing that lives shall be food for you. I have given you all things, even as the green herbs. But you shall not eat flesh with its life, that is, its blood."

—GENESIS 9:1-4

God blessed Noah and his sons as they left the ark, and the waters receded. In essence, God was saying to man that you are now in command again. In this covenant that God made with Noah, God and man were starting over. It is almost the repeat of the covenant God made with Adam giving dominion over everything to Noah. God just repeated His command, and the dominion that God gave Noah still stands today because we are descendants of Noah. When God cleansed the earth with the flood, there were eight people on the ark of God who made it through the destruction, and we are their descendants.

You are created in God's image. You not only look like God in image, but you also act like Him because you were created to fellowship with Him. To have fellowship with God, you can walk and talk with Him. You can act like Him and do the things He does. And you can hear His voice. There are limitations because of this fallen world, but God's intent was for man to enjoy fellowship with Him like in the Garden of Eden. God came down and spent time with Adam—walking, talking, and sharing close communion in the cool of the day. Ultimately, Jesus was sent to earth to redeem back the fellowship between man and God. Now, you are created in the image of God, and what He has spoken over you is a blessing just like He spoke over Adam. Notice how Genesis 1 reads:

> *So God created man in His own image; in the image of God He created him; male and female He created them. Then God blessed them, and God said to them, "Be fruitful and multiply; fill the earth and* **subdue** *it; have dominion over the fish of the sea, over the birds of the air, and over every living thing that moves on the earth."*
>
> —GENESIS 1:27-28

The word God used there is *subdue*, which means conquer. It means everything must submit to us. This idea of dominion and authority seems to be lost in Christianity today. We have become backward about the covenant and the promises of God. Yet I saw in Heaven that we are not supposed to be that way. In fact, we need to change the way we think. God created us to rule and reign—not be slaves. It is not right for human beings to be slaves or be ruled over by men who are not in the will of God. God sent Jesus Christ to redeem us! Jesus pulled us out of sin and washed us in His blood. We are redeemed and set apart from the world, and God is the One who rules over us. We must submit to God, His Spirit, and His Word.

And raised us up together, and made us sit together in the heavenly places in Christ Jesus.
—EPHESIANS 2:6

Paul is teaching that you are seated with Jesus in the heavenly realms, and you are made to have dominion and authority. Your spiritual authority over demons translates into this physical realm because demons enforce a curse and work against the will of the Lord. Angels come to enforce the blessings of God. They are hosts of Heaven who do the will of the Lord. So, if you want to rule and reign in this life, you must enforce the blessings. You must break the curses and drive out devils.

God has designed you to reign as a king in this life. God's plans and purposes are for you to dominate the devil as a child of the Most High God. You have inherited the dominion and authority of Heaven. You are to pray that the will of the Father be done on this earth as it is in Heaven. You must be disciplined in your life to accept these things that I am saying because Jesus came to seek and save those who were lost. He came to retrieve people, to deliver people, and to heal people, and you are supposed to do the same. You are supposed to rescue souls from the devil and take back what the devil stole.

You must live a disciplined life so you do not get caught up in the devil's traps. You must remain separate from the world and live an upright life in Christ Jesus. Just say "no" to the flesh at all times because your flesh is how the devil tries to entrap you. You must not fear because fear is torment and domination, but you are full of God. God is love, and in Him there is no fear only perfect love, which drives out fear (see 1 John 4:18).

Fear is a spirit, and Paul told Timothy that we are not to have a spirit of fear but of love and of power and of a sound mind (see 2 Timothy 1:7).

THE WARFARE OF THE MIND

Jesus purchased you, redeemed you, restored your authority, and that is what you need to concentrate on now. Be disciplined, focused, and meditate on these truths. Through Jesus Christ, you have been restored to the original relationship that God had with Adam. While you are on this earth, you must deal with your body and mind that are not redeemed, and you have warfare to do.

> *For the weapons of our warfare are not carnal but mighty in God for pulling down strongholds, casting down arguments and every high thing that exalts itself against the knowledge of God, bringing every thought into captivity to the obedience of Christ.*
>
> —2 CORINTHIANS 10:4-5

Demons that have stopped you from hearing from God will now have to flee. They have been the ones who have stopped you from hearing God's voice. You are a child of God, and Jesus said His sheep hear His voice (see John 10:27). As Christians, we always hear God's voice because He is our Shepherd. Jesus said we hear His voice, so we can! It is the demonic warfare down here on earth that tries to keep you out of the place where you can hear from God. But they are fleeing right now in the name of Jesus! All the warfare and all the attacks you have encountered are diminishing now because the power of the Lord Jesus Christ is coming into your life.

Angels of the Lord are camping around you and creating an atmosphere for you to hear from your heavenly Father. Stand firm and refuse to accept anything contrary to God's Word and will. As a child of God, you have ears that hear and eyes that see. Sometimes you just need to open the Bible and let God speak to you that way because the Bible is the Word of God; the Bible is the will of God. God is producing in you every good thing, and He is doing it by depositing the Word of God—His incorruptible seed—in you.

Let me remind you that warfare is not against flesh and blood or warring against people. You are to cast down arguments or anything contrary or anything that tries to exalt itself against the knowledge of God. I just want to re-emphasize this verse in Second Corinthians, because it is so important.

> For the weapons of our warfare are not carnal but mighty in God for pulling down strongholds, casting down arguments and every high thing that exalts itself against the knowledge of God, bringing every thought into captivity to the obedience of Christ.
>
> 2 CORINTHIANS 10:4-5

Spiritual warfare is not about you wrestling with demons physically or spiritually. A demon cannot have power over you if you do not let him into your thought process. Once a demon gets into your mind, he can get into your body. If you are a born-again Christian, a demon cannot get into your spirit, but it still can control you by how much power you have given it over you. So don't let the enemy have any power over you. Come against anything that exalts itself against the knowledge of God. As this verse says, you must bring every thought into captivity to the obedience of Christ. In other words, discipline your soulish realm. This is very important to grasp because your spiritual warfare also has to do with your mind and your body. Your spirit is not the only contact point with the spiritual realm, your mind and your body are also, and that is where the devil tries to get in.

You must be rough and forceful with the devil and never give him any leeway. You must be strong against him. Do not let the devil dominate you; you dominate the devil. Make the devil the victim by resisting him, pushing him back, and being rough with him. Then you need to pull down those strongholds in prayer. Any false ideas you have must go by having your mind transformed, which comes by renewing your mind with the Word of God (see Romans 12:2). In the name of Jesus, you must come against anything that is opposite to the Word of God. This is true spiritual warfare.

Jesus came to this earth in the image of man, and yet, He is God. Jesus walked on this earth and operated in two realms—the heavenly realm and the earthly realm. He is our example of how to live on earth; He showed us how to do it. Jesus was crucified, He redeemed us, went back to the Father, and the Holy Spirit was sent to earth to empower us. Jesus cleared the way for us to walk in power through the Holy Spirit.

Jesus only acted on the will of the Father. It was God's will to rule and reign over demons through Jesus. It was God's will for Jesus to live and move and have His being in the Father and for Jesus to do mighty miracles (see John 5:19). But it is also God's will that you live and move and have your being in Him (see Acts 17:28) and that *you* move in miracles, signs, and wonders (see Mark 16:17-20). It is the Father's will that *you* walk in authority, that *you* have dominion, and that *you* see the Kingdom of God come forth in a very powerful way.

God knows your name and has already written a book about you. God has already considered everything about you. He wrote your days in that book before one of them came to pass. Before you were even born, He had already considered you, designed your life, and planned everything through for you. He wrote this wonderful book about you, and He is thinking of you right now. God wants to accomplish everything He already planned for you and is written in Heaven in your books.

There is nothing impossible to you! No matter what the circumstances are right now in your life or how contrary they seem, it does not matter. God has already written about you, and you need to stand on what God's Word says. Your life is different now because Jesus Christ came into your life. He has changed the way you think and the way you respond to things. He has intervened in your life, and because of that, limitations have been removed. Now it is your turn to remove the limitations on others by telling them about the gospel of Jesus Christ.

Once you overthrow evil spirits harassing you, you can minister to others the same freedom you have and drive devils out of their lives. You can watch people change and respond to the environment of Heaven because demon spirits are no longer influencing them. Most people do not establish the battleground in their own lives and rid themselves of demonic forces. They feel hindered all the time in ministry, but true ministry is when you are free first and then go out and minister to others.

A Yielded and Disciplined Lifestyle

For the word of God is living and powerful, and sharper than any two-edged sword, piercing even to the division of soul and spirit, and of joints and marrow, and is a discerner of the thoughts and intents of the heart.

—Hebrews 4:12

You have the Word of God dividing between what is spiritual and what is soulish and dividing between the thoughts and intents of the heart like surgery. God's Word will show you what is of Him and what is of you and what is of the soul and what is of the spirit. The Word of God is that powerful—that sharp!

When you are born again, the Sword that is the Word of the Lord begins separating and discerning. This doesn't happen in your head but in your heart. The Spirit of God wants you to see clearly what is of Him and what is of the devil or even your flesh. The Spirit of God wants to open your spiritual eyes, and He does this inside of you.

Sometimes your mind, will, and emotions work against God, and that is why you need to have the Word of God operating in your life. The Sword of the Spirit is the Word of God. You must pray in the Spirit, pray in tongues, and build yourself up, and then meditate on the Word of God. This practice will cause you to grow and mature, and the voice of your spirit will get louder and louder. The voice of your spirit is connected to the voice of God, and when you join yourself to the Lord you become one with Him in Spirit.

> *But he who is joined to the Lord is one spirit with*
> *Him.*
> —1 CORINTHIANS 6:17

Your body might not respond, but your spirit will respond to the voice of God. The Word of God will separate what is of your spirit and what is of your soul. Hearing God's voice becomes a lot easier when you educate your mind, will, and emotions and discipline your body according to God's Word. It quiets the different influences that pull you away from the original voice of God down deep in your heart and discerned by your spirit. In this process, you start to rule and reign as you hear the voice of your Father and eliminate all the other voices. You will discern rightly because the Word of God and the Spirit of God become evident in your life.

> *I have been crucified with Christ; it is no longer I*
> *who live, but Christ lives in me; and the life which*
> *I now live in the flesh I live by faith in the Son of*
> *God, who loved me and gave Himself for me.*
> —GALATIANS 2:20

Here in Galatians, the apostle Paul is talking about the crucified life and how he was crucified with Christ. He said he no longer lived, but Christ lived in him. If you're not hearing God's voice, this Scripture may help you understand why. Have you crucified your flesh? Are you living the crucified life?

> *I assure you, believers, by the pride which I have*
> *in you in [your union with] Christ Jesus our Lord,*
> *I die daily [I face death and die to self].*
> —1 CORINTHIANS 15:31 AMP

Paul said he faces death to himself daily, and because of that, he was able to be an apostle, an effective vessel on this earth. Paul is saying that in your union with Christ, you also can take upon yourself the death of Jesus and the life of Jesus. They both can work in you. That life he's talking about is the resurrection power of Jesus Christ. You must learn to yield to the crucified life, which means saying "no" to ungodliness and worldly passions.

> *Take my yoke upon you. Let me teach you, because*
> *I am humble and gentle at heart, and you will*
> *find rest for your souls.*
> —MATTHEW 11:29 NLT

Jesus gave you His yoke and wants you to live a disciplined life yielded to God's will and not your own. He wants you to put His yoke upon yourself so He can teach you how to walk in the Spirit in this life. In other words, you will "no" to the flesh and say "yes" to the Holy Spirit. Then the Spirit of God can lead you into all truth, and that is what the Holy Spirit does.

However, when He, the Spirit of truth, has come, He will guide you into all truth; for He will not speak on His own authority, but whatever He hears He will speak; and He will tell you things to come.

—John 16:13

I believe the Spirit of God is speaking to you and leading you even now. Many times, there are just minor adjustments that you need to make daily in order to walk with God. Then before you know it, things clean up in your life and you begin to hear the voice of God in a stronger way. Keep in mind that you must have an intensity to push back at the devil and be rough with him to overthrow him. Never forget that God's intention for man is to rule, reign, and dominate—not be a victim.

A Story

Years ago, my wife, Kathi, and I declared war on financial debt in our lives. We took authority over it in the name of Jesus every chance we could. I could sense the authority in the Spirit as we spoke the powerful name of Jesus to our circumstances.

As we continued in our giving, worked hard, and controlled our spending, God began to help us financially. We were astonished at the resistance we encountered in the spirit over this endeavor to become debt free. It felt like we were doing hand-to-hand combat with hordes of evil entities that did not want us to be free.

But as we persistently endured, breakthroughs began to happen with financial miracles coming one after another. We had finally dethroned evil spirits who were enforcing a curse in our lives. Even though Jesus has already dethroned these principalities and powers, Kathi and I had to learn to enforce our victory with spiritual warfare using the name of Jesus.

I ended up getting extra hours at work in overtime pay. I would be offered more work than I could handle. My company also gave me raise after raise in pay and benefits over a ten-year period. Finally, someone left us money to pay off our house mortgage after we had just paid off our automobile. We now live debt free and never desire to go back to debt. We learned to walk in our authority and dominion, and you can too!

Chapter 6

THE ROLE OF THE HOLY SPIRIT

Now may the God of peace Himself sanctify
you completely; and may your whole spirit,
soul, and body be preserved blameless at
the coming of our Lord Jesus Christ.

—1 THESSALONIANS 5:23

AS WE'VE DISCUSSED IN EARLIER CHAPTERS, YOU ARE A three-part being. You are an eternal spirit who has a body, which is your earth suit. You also have a soul, which is your mind, will, and emotions. When you are born again, the Spirit of God comes to dwell in your spirit, and you become a new creature in Christ Jesus. However, the changes needed in your soul and body are not automatic, and you will need to work on them.

In fact, there are many challenges your soul and body will encounter in this realm down here on the earth. Emotionally, physically, and psychologically you will encounter things that are contrary to God's will for your life on earth. Your mind, will, and emotions are not redeemed, and you will need to transform them by renewing your mind to the Word of God. Your physical body also encounters things down here that are contrary to the Word of God and the will of God. You will have to discipline your body by telling it what to do because it will not just do the right thing automatically. It will need to be disciplined according to the Word of God.

The real miracle occurs in your born-again spirit. *"Therefore, if anyone is in Christ, he is a new creation; old things have passed away; behold, all things have become new"* (2 Corinthians 5:17). At the new birth, your spirit is not just changed. It is made instantly and completely new, and the Spirit of God comes to live and make His home on the inside of you.

> *In the beginning God created the heavens and the earth. The earth was without form, and void; and darkness was on the face of the deep. And the Spirit of God was hovering over the face of the waters.*
> —GENESIS 1:1-2

In the beginning, when the earth was still void, the Spirit of God hovered over the face of the deep. The Holy Spirit was there in the creation and was executing the commands of the Father from Heaven over the earth and forming God's creation. You can see here that the Holy Spirit is a Creator, and that is why you know that you have been created in the image of God. Through Jesus Christ, the Holy Spirit came and restored God's original intent back for you, and you have become a new creature in Christ. The Trinity was in the formation of the earth, and the Trinity was in the formation of man.

As a born-again Christian, you now have the role of the Holy Spirit in your life. It is very interesting how many people do not understand what happens in their lives when they become born-again. It is partially because they do not understand how they are made up. You may not have known that you have three parts (spirit, soul, body) to you. You may not have understood that the Holy Spirit will not influence you in your body or your mind. The Holy Spirit will talk to you and influence you in *your spirit* because that is where the Holy Spirit dwells in you.

God framed the world through spiritual words. God is a Spirit, and He spoke the words of creation, and creation appeared in the physical world. There was a transference from what is in Heaven to this physical realm. It is the same way with the Holy Spirit inside of you. When you preach the Word of God through the power of the Holy Spirit, you physically have to speak the spiritual words. When those words come into this earthly environment, signs and wonders confirm the Word of God (see Mark 16:20). There must be that manifestation of the sons of God and the manifestation of signs and wonders when you preach the Word.

It all began at creation. The Holy Spirit was very important in the creation and the framing of the world and is very important in your life when you are born again of the Spirit. The Holy Spirit will never leave you, and He will stay with you continually. He is in your midst right now. Not only is the Holy Spirit in you, but He is upon you. God anoints you with the Holy

Spirit, and He sings songs of deliverance over you (see Psalm 32:7). When you are sleeping, God is speaking words over you. The Holy Spirit is in you speaking words, and the anointing of God on you is constantly reminding you of what God has said.

> *The Lord your God in your midst, the Mighty One, will save; He will rejoice over you with gladness, He will quiet you with His love, He will rejoice over you with singing.*
> —ZEPHANIAH 3:17

Zephaniah describes in these verses what the Holy Spirit does in your life. Jesus said that the Comforter would come, and when He does, He would wrap you up in God's love. The Holy Spirit is your Advocate, Helper, Counselor. He will never leave you, but He will be with you forever. It is also through the Holy Spirit that God will communicate with you. God wants to speak to you all the time, and the Holy Spirit is the one God uses to do that. Your spirit is where the communication happens between you and God on this earth. It is through the Holy Spirit who dwells within your spirit that God will speak to you. God does not speak to you through your mind. Thoughts can come from anywhere; you get them all the time, but the Holy Spirit is the central Person that communicates with you in this realm on earth because that is what He was sent by God to do for you.

ABLE TO HEAR GOD'S VOICE

When you understand that God is a Spirit, you will understand how God speaks to you through your spirit. When you are born again, you are renewed with the life of God, and you are receptive now to God's voice because the life of God is in you. It is not unusual to hear God's voice. Most people think it is rare to hear God's voice, but as a child of God, you are supposed to hear the voice of your Father in Heaven. You are supposed to hear the voice of your Shepherd, the Great Shepherd Jesus Christ. It should not be considered unusual or a rare occasion that you hear from God. You are supposed to be able to communicate and be led by the Holy Spirit.

> *For as many as are led by the Spirit of God, these are sons of God.*
>
> —ROMANS 8:14

Those who are led by the Spirit are children of God. God speaks to you through your inner man, and it is something spiritual that happens. God speaks in an intimate voice deep in your spirit. It is not a loud voice necessarily, but it is a sure voice that matches what the Word of God has already said to you. You need to silence the other voices in your life and eliminate the chatter. When you can start to eliminate wrong voices by discernment, then God's voice will become even clearer and louder to you. At times, you will have to control your environment and how much worldly input you allow in your life. You need to take time to shut yourself off so that you can be quiet before the Lord. Start with ten minutes per day, and gradually try to get up to an hour. This is time that you dedicate to God and allow Him to talk to you.

The Seed that Grows

But He answered and said, "It is written, 'Man shall not live by bread alone, but by every word that proceeds from the mouth of God.'"

—Matthew 4:4

You should be hungry to eat the Word of God every day because that is God speaking to you. There is a transference that happens when you read the Word of God and then meditate on it. It goes down into your spirit and actually turns into a substance that expands inside of you. The seed of the Word of God grows inside of you when you meditate on it day and night. It is this process that allows the Word of God to become dimensional inside of you and become living and active. You are now *receiving* the Word of God into your life.

> *It is the Spirit who gives life; the flesh profits nothing. The words that I speak to you are spirit, and they are life.*
>
> —John 6:63

In this verse, Jesus was telling the people that His Words are spirit and life. I am sure some who were there listening were hearing Jesus speak as just a person. However, Jesus was telling them that they were not just hearing His physical voice but that His words are life and spirit as well. There is a transference from the spirit realm to the physical realm, and the Words that God speaks are part of that transference.

> *I am the living bread which came down from heaven. If anyone eats of this bread, he will live forever; and the bread that I shall give is My flesh, which I shall give for the life of the world.*
>
> —JOHN 6:51

Jesus is claiming that His flesh is the living bread, and anyone who eats this bread will live forever. You have eternal life because Jesus offered Himself up for you. He is the bread that came down from Heaven. You need to allow your mind to be transformed and renewed by these truths.

One day Jesus looked at the crowd that was following Him in the heat of the day. They had already been fed by the miracle that fed five thousand (see Matthew 14:13-21). They also had seen other miracles, but they really did not hear or believe Jesus was the Messiah. Jesus discerned their unbelief and told them they needed to eat His flesh and drink His blood or they could have no part in Him (see John 6:53). Jesus was trying to tell them He had to become their source. These people were being entertained by the manifestations in His ministry and were not committed to Him.

You can learn a lesson here by meditating on the fact that Jesus is the Living Bread, and He is the Bread that came down from Heaven. Once you read this verse and meditate on it, it is absorbed into your life, and your mind also becomes renewed. Allow your spirit to become strong to the point where it rules over your body. Do not give yourself over to the works of the flesh. Get to the place where you can tell your body what to do and not let your body tell you what to do. Paul said that those who walk in the flesh are enemies of God because the war is between your flesh and your spirit (see Romans 8:4-8). As you walk closer to God, understand that your spirit man and the Spirit of God are one. You are walking with God and your spirit or our inner man is also walking close to God, It is because of the born-again experience and the baptism of the Holy Spirit that causes you to overcome the flesh and the mind.

The Holy Spirit will reveal to you what the Father's heart is. He will take that which is spiritual and reveal it to you (see 1 Corinthians 2:6-16). The Holy Spirit will remind you of what Jesus said, and He will remind you of what's ahead (see John 14:26). He will tell you the future, but He will also remind you of things that have already been spoken (see John 16:13). The Holy Spirit will continue to remind you of the truth written in Heaven about you. Angels read the books about you, and they come down to earth and enforce what God has written there.

You need to agree with God and allow Him to come into your life in a greater way by allowing the Holy Spirit's power to become predominant in your spirit. Then you must say "no" to your flesh and "no" to thoughts contrary to what God has for you. Do not allow your mind to control you. You must allow your mind to be transformed and think and meditate on those things that are from above.

ENCOUNTERING THE SPIRIT REALM

You encounter this physical realm all the time because you are living here, but unfortunately, very few of us encounter the spiritual realm because we don't recognize that we are spiritual beings. You can try to be spiritual and try to do things you think are spiritual activities, but it is really about yielding to the Holy Spirit than anything else. It is about crucifying the flesh and allowing your mind to think on the things that are set above (see Colossians 3:2-10). The truth about Heaven needs to be the reality of your life. There are realities and truths in Heaven that need to come into your life. Once you allow the Holy Spirit to be the predominant Person in your life through your spirit, you will start to hear the voice of the Lord like never before!

Your mind, will, and emotions need to bend and submit to the will of God. They need to be transformed and obey what God has said (see Romans 12:2-3). Your mind, will, and emotions must accept the truth of God, and then the Holy Spirit will fit them within the framework of what God's Word says. They must completely bow to the will of God, and this happens through revelation. When the Holy Spirit comes in, He gives you revelation and illuminates and ignites truth to you. When this happens, it becomes very clear to you in that moment—it is a supernatural event. Your mind can be changed permanently if you allow the revelation to rework and rewire your thinking and let this realm of the Holy Spirit become dominant in your life.

But when the Helper (Comforter, Advocate, Intercessor—Counselor, Strengthener, Standby) comes,

*whom I will send to you from the Father, that is
the Spirit of Truth who comes from the Father,
He will testify and bear witness about Me.*
—JOHN 15:26 AMP

Here in these verses is a good description of the Holy
Spirit's role in your life. He will intercede for you. The Holy
Spirit will open your eyes and show you the truth (see John
16:13). This truth comes from the Father in Heaven, and it
is He who sent Jesus and the Holy Spirit. The Holy Spirit is
the revealer of truth and the third Person of the Holy Trinity.
The Holy Spirit is the one who carried out God's command
to create the universe in Genesis, and the same Holy Spirit is
now in you. He has made you a new creation in Christ, but
He is also within you to comfort you and be an Advocate for
you. The Holy Spirit is within you to be your Counselor, your
Strength, and your Standby.

THE COMFORTER

The Holy Spirit will testify and bear witness of everything Jesus
said. Remember that the Comforter's plan is to wrap you up and
make you feel safe. He will comfort you in circumstances that
are contrary to what you should be enduring. You will feel like
you are in a bad dream at times because this world is not like
Heaven, but the Holy Spirit will comfort you in these contrary
circumstances. Allow Him to do that for you! He will assure
you that victory is yours, it is on the way, and a breakthrough is
coming. He will remind you of what Jesus said.

...God, who gives life to the dead and calls those things which do not exist as though they did.

—ROMANS 4:17

The Holy Spirit will tell you the end from the beginning. He will tell you that everything will work out. If you look and focus on your circumstances, you can get discouraged so focus on the fact that you have provision and security with Jesus Christ. The Holy Spirit in you is more than a conqueror, and He is the one who will put you over (see Romans 8:37). *"All things work together for good for those who love God and are called according to His purpose"* (see Romans 8:28).

When you receive the Holy Spirit as your Comforter, He will encourage you! What He says will sometimes be the opposite of what you are encountering, but He will tell you about all the good things God is doing and how everything will turn out all right. He will always assure you that victory is yours in Jesus Christ!

THE COUNSELOR

The Holy Spirit is also a Counselor, and He will come to you and talk to you and can tell you what you should do in any given circumstance. We call this understanding or wisdom, and it is one of the things that the Holy Spirit was sent to do for you. The Holy Spirit is *full* of the wisdom and counsel of God, and He wants to implement the will of God into your life if you let Him. He will come as a Counselor and impart wisdom and counsel, but you must let Him speak to you. The Spirit of God wants to speak to you, and you *can* hear God's voice. The Holy

Spirit will speak wisdom to you and speak the understanding of things to you that you did not have. He will give you revelation deep in your spirit because as a born-again Christian you have the Counselor living within you.

Remember that God speaks to you in your spirit, and the understanding you seek is also received in your spirit. What He speaks will come up into your mind, and then you can exercise whatever actions are needed in your flesh. But spiritually it all begins in your spirit and then manifests itself in the flesh because you and the Holy Spirit communicate Spirit to spirit.

THE HELPER

The Holy Spirit is also your Helper, and the Helper wants to come alongside you and implement what God is saying. Not only does God speak to you, but He also wants to bring it to pass. God, in His mercy, has given you a Standby who never leaves you. The Holy Spirit will carry out God's plans for your life. Part of God's voice will be physical manifestation, but it will be through the Holy Spirit giving you guidance in every situation.

> *For you did not receive the spirit of bondage again to fear, but you received the Spirit of adoption by whom we cry out, "Abba, Father." The Spirit Himself bears witness with our spirit that we are children of God.*
>
> —ROMANS 8:15-16

Jesus said that He would not leave you as an orphan because the Holy Spirit would be with you (see John 14:18-24). You have been given the Holy Spirit, who is a Helper who will be there for you and assist you. Never let yourself fear anything in your life because there is bondage in fear. Paul told Timothy that he was not to give way to a spirit of fear. *"For God has not given us a spirit of fear, but of power and of love and of a sound mind"* (2 Timothy 1:7). God gave you the spirit of love and power and a sound mind.

THE ADVOCATE

The word *Advocate* is used for the Holy Spirit. Advocate is a legal term that refers to a lawyer who takes up your case and helps you beyond what you can do. The Advocate helps you in your weaknesses. When you need someone to help you, your Advocate is there. The Holy Spirit helps you pray and give voice to what you need to pray out to God.

> *Likewise the Spirit also helps in our weaknesses.*
> *For we do not know what we should pray for as we*
> *ought, but the Spirit Himself makes intercession*
> *for us with groanings which cannot be uttered.*
> —ROMANS 8:26

In your weakness, the Spirit helps you pray out the perfect will of God with perfect prayers that you could not utter on your own because He is an Advocate. He is like a lawyer that wants to take the case that seems to be against you and turn it around. He knows you can win your case. God wants you to yield right now to your Advocate, the mighty Advocate, the Holy Spirit.

THE STRENGTHENER

The Spirit of God who raised Jesus from the dead is also *your* Strengthener. The Holy Spirit raised Lazarus from the dead, and the Holy Spirit was the one who raised Jesus from the dead. That is how strong He is. Paul said that the same power that raised Jesus from the dead dwells in you. That is the kind of strength the Spirit of God has inside of you.

> *But if the Spirit of Him who raised Jesus from the dead dwells in you, He who raised Christ from the dead will also give life to your mortal bodies through His Spirit who dwells in you.*
>
> —ROMANS 8:11

Paul said the Spirit of God in you will quicken, make alive, and give life to your mortal body. The Holy Spirit will ignite your spirit, and this will affect your physical body. The Strengthener will help you psychologically and cause your mind to align with the will of God. The Holy Spirit will help you in your mind, with your emotions and your will and cause you to bend to God's will. He will give you the strength to stand up and do the right thing. You will gain understanding because the Holy Spirit strengthens you from the inside and in your understanding. You must hand yourself over to Him and hear the voice of the Lord speaking loud and clear inside of you.

> *But you, beloved, building yourselves up on your most holy faith, praying in the Holy Spirit, keep*

yourselves in the love of God, looking for the mercy
of our Lord Jesus Christ unto eternal life.

—JUDE 1:20-21

The Holy Spirit will keep you right in line with God's will and keep you right where the strength is. This is what will happen when your mind aligns with the will of God. Your spirit will be free to rule and reign. Your mind will line up with God's will and side with your spirit. When this happens, then the Holy Spirit will be able to take you where you need to go.

THE STANDBY

The Holy Spirit as Standby began in Genesis. The Spirit of God was hovering over the face of the deep, and He was on standby until God the Father spoke everything into creation. I saw this when I was in Heaven. The Holy Spirit was hovering over the waters, God the Father spoke, and the Holy Spirit accomplished it. It is the same with you! The Holy Spirit is waiting to do many things for you. He is on standby right now for you, and He is waiting for the will of God to be implemented in your life. The Standby is waiting because what He is able to get done for you has to do with you and your communication with God.

The Holy Spirit and angels are always on standby to make sure that you get everything written about you in your books in Heaven. The Standby ignites your spirit. He uses the command from Heaven to resound in your spirit, and the angels obey. The angels are always considering what your personal book in Heaven says about you.

Everything that God has for you, you can have on this earth when you obey and speak forth what God is saying. The angels start to work as you bring forth the spirit of prophecy and yield to the Holy Spirit. When you yield to the Holy Spirit and prophesy, things start to be framed and happen in the heavenly realm.

The only hope that you have as a born-again Christian on the earth is the Holy Spirit. You have redemption through the blood of Jesus Christ and everything you need for life and godliness (see 2 Peter 1:3). In this earthly realm, you have to rely solely on the Spirit of God; He is your only hope.

You must implement all of these characteristics of the Holy Spirit into your life. Meditate on these characteristics of God and the characteristics of the Holy Spirit. God wants you to have everything He has already planned for you, and He wants you to hear His voice. The Holy Spirit must become predominant in your life for you to hear God's voice.

A STORY

One way to allow the Spirit to become predominant in your life is to have consistent, set times in the presence of God. During these special times, you should implement worship, meditation of the Word of God, and praying in the Spirit. After I have accomplished these, I begin to yield to the Spirit of prophecy and verbally confirm what the Lord is saying for this time in my life. Many Scriptures should flow from your lips as they come up out of your spirit. Over the years of doing this routine as often as possible, the Holy Spirit has been able to speak to me in extraordinary ways.

I remember one particular person I would pray for multiple times a day with the guidance of the Holy Spirit. I had seen a picture of the person previously, and the Holy Spirit would continually bring the person's face before me and start to intercede on the person's behalf through me. One early morning, the Holy Spirit woke me up at 2:00 a.m. to have me pray for this particular individual. This had been the second or third time in a row. I saw that this individual had such a call on her life, and He was going to use her in a mighty way to make history for the Kingdom of God. I had never met her, but as the Holy Spirit was briefing me on all of this, I simply said to Him, "Why don't You just send her to my next conference? I will tell her all of these wonderful things myself and impart what is on me to her?"

Later that next week, I was speaking in that conference. As I walked out onto the stage and looked out at the crowd, there on the second row was the person I had prayed for daily for the past two months! At the end of the last session of the conference, I called her up and prophesied and imparted everything that was to come upon her. The power of God came and touched her while she was in her seat before I could even lay hands on her. Several days before, this person said that she knew she had to get to the conference, which matched the time I told the Lord to bring her to the meeting.

This encounter shows you how the Holy Spirit can speak to us and coordinate the will of God for our lives in a supernatural manner.

Chapter 7

THE BREATH OF GOD

*The wind blows where it wishes, and you hear the
sound of it, but cannot tell where it comes from and
where it goes. So is everyone who is born of the Spirit.*

—JOHN 3:8

JESUS WAS TALKING TO NICODEMUS, AND HE DESCRIBED
the Spirit of God as being like the wind. Jesus explained that
we cannot see the Spirit of God, but we can see the effects of
the Spirit just like we see effects of the wind blowing the tree
branches. The wind is invisible, but the power of the wind can
be seen. In the same way, we cannot see the Spirit of God, but
we can see His manifestations.

*Nicodemus said to Him, "How can a man be
born when he is old? Can he enter a second time
into his mother's womb and be born?" Jesus
answered, "Most assuredly, I say to you, unless one*

is born of water and the Spirit, he cannot enter the Kingdom of God. That which is born of the flesh is flesh, and that which is born of the Spirit is spirit. Do not marvel that I said to you, 'You must be born again.' The wind blows where it wishes, and you hear the sound of it, but cannot tell where it comes from and where it goes. So is everyone who is born of the Spirit."

—JOHN 3:4-8

You may not see the Holy Spirit, but His touch will change you, and you will respond. You will see the effects of the Spirit in your life.

Jesus answered and said to him, "Most assuredly, I say to you, unless one is born again, he cannot see the Kingdom of God."

—JOHN 3:3

Unless you are born again, you cannot see the Kingdom of God, and that born-again experience is talking about the breath of God. God breathes on you through the Holy Spirit, and He causes you to become a new creation in Christ Jesus (see 2 Corinthians 5:17).

RECEIVING THE BREATH OF GOD

By which have been given to us exceedingly great and precious promises, that through these you may

be partakers of the divine nature, having escaped
the corruption that is in the world through lust.
—2 PETER 1:4

You have been given everything you need for life and godliness through God's promises, and you can be a partaker of
the divine nature. Here, Peter is telling you that you have been
given things that have been spoken by God. God's promises are
His Word, and if He promised it to you, then He wants to give
it to you. Because you become a partaker of God's nature—the
divine nature—you can escape whatever corruption is in the
world. That is a profound statement. Through Jesus Christ, you
can overcome the world!

You have to back away from the voices which are from the
spirit of this world. Everything about this world and the world
system speaks, and you need to tune those voices out and back
away from them. You need to tell your soul to be quiet so that
your spirit, which is filled with the Holy Spirit, can be heard.
God wants to help you in whatever situation you find yourself.
He wants to do that by helping you be empowered while you
are here on this earth. By God giving you His promises, you can
escape the corruption that is in the world caused by lust.

And when He had said this, He breathed on
them, and said to them, "Receive the Holy Spirit."
—JOHN 20:22

Jesus physically breathed on the disciples. When He did
this, it was to show them that His breath was the Holy Spirit
because He said, *"Receive the Holy Spirit."* When He breathed

the breath of God on them, He was saying, "Receive My breath." You can receive Jesus' breath right now, and that breath is the same breath that created life. The same breath that Jesus breathed out is the same breath that He breathed out into Adam's nostrils when He made him.

> *Then the Lord God formed [that is, created the body of] man from the dust of the ground, and breathed into his nostrils the breath of life; and the man became a living being [an individual complete in body and spirit].*
>
> —GENESIS 2:7 AMP

The same breath that God breathed into man when he was created is the same breath that caused you to be born again of the Spirit of God. The breath of God is also part of God's voice, and this establishes the fact that God's breath can be His voice as well. The breath of God is breathing on you, and He is forming words and speaking His promises to you.

> *And I looked, and behold, there were sinews on the bones, and flesh grew and skin covered them; but there was no breath in them. Then He said to me, "Prophesy to the breath, son of man, and say to the breath, 'Thus says the Lord God, "Come from the four winds, O breath, and breathe on these slain, that they may live."'" So I prophesied as He commanded me, and the breath came into them, and they came to life and stood up on their feet, an exceedingly great army.*
>
> —EZEKIEL 37:8-10 AMP

God can speak to you in different ways, and He does not need to necessarily use words. In this case, it was God's breath that came out and into the people who were dead, and they became alive. It was through the prophet's breath, but it was God who commanded Ezekiel to prophesy. You can see here the process of prophesy. You can see that there are Words that have breath, and the breath came back into the people when the prophet prophesied by the Spirit of God.

> *And they were all filled with the Holy Spirit and began to speak with other tongues, as the Spirit gave them utterance.*
>
> —ACTS 2:4

God can speak to you in different ways. When you prophesy, you are speaking by the Spirit as He gives you utterance. When that happens, you are speaking from the spirit realm originating in Heaven. The spirit of prophecy is the testimony of Jesus Christ (see Revelation 19:10).

> *God is Spirit, and those who worship Him must worship in spirit and truth.*
>
> —JOHN 4:24

God's voice is activated inside of your spirit because God is a Spirit, and those who worship Him must worship Him in spirit and in truth. A true prophet allows God to speak through him or her, and what God speaks through the prophet is God's word. God's word comes forth, and it is a living thing. When you speak forth, you should speak as though you are speaking the very oracles of God.

If anyone speaks, let him speak as the oracles of God. If anyone ministers, let him do it as with the ability which God supplies, that in all things God may be glorified through Jesus Christ, to whom belong the glory and the dominion forever and ever. Amen.

—1 PETER 4:11

Peter is talking about the revelations of God, and this is very important to understand. You are supposed to yield to the Holy Spirit, to the breath of God, and speak forth. God will give you the ability to speak as the Spirit supplies so in all things you will glorify God. This Scripture is talking about your life down here on this earth and how you need to draw deeply from what God is saying. Then when you speak forth God's word, you should speak as an oracle of God.

Pursue love, and desire spiritual gifts, but especially that you may prophesy. For he who speaks in a tongue does not speak to men but to God, for no one understands him; however, in the spirit he speaks mysteries. But he who prophesies speaks edification and exhortation and comfort to men.

—1 CORINTHIANS 14:1-3

Paul said that you should desire spiritual gifts. He said especially desire that you should prophesy because it is prophecy that edifies the body. When you prophesy, you are speaking out in the known language of the people, and it edifies them because they hear and understand it. If you speak in tongues in the church, you are not speaking to men but to God, and people will not understand what you are saying.

If you are born again and baptized in the Holy Spirit, you can speak in tongues and ask God for the interpretation of what is being said. The Holy Spirit wants to speak through you more than you know. If the resurrection power that raised Jesus from the dead is dwelling in you, then that power will quicken your mortal body. That is when the Holy Spirit will take your tongue and use it. Do not limit the Holy Spirit, but let Him speak and move through you. Let the breath of God continually come through you—not just upon you. The resurrection power that is in you wants to do God's will, which agrees with God's Spirit and His Word.

You can raise people from the dead, heal the sick, drive out devils, and speak in new tongues (see Matthew 10:8). You can preach and testify of Jesus wherever you go, and that is what God wants you to do by yielding to the breath of God. God is always speaking because there are always things going on in Heaven. God's Word that was spoken many years ago is still being spoken today, and spiritually it is still going through the atmosphere.

God wants you to yield to His Spirit and speak into your world. That is His will for you. God wants to do exceedingly and abundantly above what you could ever ask or think (see Ephesians 3:20). God wants to use you to influence this earthly realm. Did you know that you can change a generation, and you can actually make history? The way that you do that is by yielding to the breath of God Almighty. God does not want you to wait on Him any longer. He wants you to yield to Him and then jump into what He is calling you to do. God is waiting for you to come to the place where you will know His perfect will. I have seen the breath of God influence so many people to the point where their blinders are taken off. They start to hear the voice of God as they have never heard before because the breath of God has resurrection power in it.

> *So also is the resurrection of the dead. The body is sown in corruption, it is raised in incorruption. It is sown in dishonor, it is raised in glory. It is sown in weakness, it is raised in power. It is sown a natural body, it is raised a spiritual body. There is a natural body, and there is a spiritual body. And so it is written, "The first man Adam became a living being." The last Adam became a life-giving spirit.*
>
> —1 CORINTHIANS 15:42-45

The first Adam was created. God breathed into him, and Adam became a living soul. The last Adam, Jesus Christ, is a life-giving Spirit. He is perpetual, and there will not be another. He is continually giving life from God the Father. The life-giving Spirit, the Holy Spirit, is inside of you, and He will speak to you and *through* you. He is quickening you even now as you are reading this. You can sense the resurrection power of the Holy Spirit because He is the Life-Giver. He is forming words inside of you, and you need to speak them out.

> *Then Moses said to him, "Are you zealous for my sake? Oh, that all the Lord's people were prophets*

and that the Lord would put His Spirit upon them!"

—NUMBERS 11:29

A young man ran to Moses to tell him that two men in the camp were prophesying, even though they had not been at the tabernacle. Moses answered and said he wished that all of Israel would prophesy. In the New Testament, Paul said he wished that everyone would desire the greater spiritual gifts, especially that you may prophesy. God wants you to yield to the Spirit and begin to speak out.

> *But the hour is coming, and now is, when the true worshipers will worship the Father in spirit and truth; for the Father is seeking such to worship Him. God is Spirit, and those who worship Him must worship in spirit and truth."*

—JOHN 4:23-24

When you pray in the Spirit, you are accessing the supernatural and connecting yourself with God and His ways. This relationship that you have with God will cause things to change in this realm! As soon as you put words to what the Spirit is saying, it becomes a transaction in this physical realm. You can be praying in the Spirit, and God will influence you through the Spirit of God by giving you words within you. When you speak God's word out, it causes a transaction, a manifestation in the physical realm.

Your words are powerful, and that is why you need to watch your words. You are taking something that you cannot see and making it known in this realm through God's words. As you allow God to breathe on you, words will form that you must speak out. How supernatural it is that you will bring forth something from the spiritual realm into the physical realm. Praying in tongues and prophesying are supernatural events that your Father in Heaven wants you to have. You can have all these things in the privacy of your own home in your prayer life.

YOUR FUTURE IN GOD'S HANDS

You should yield to the Spirit of prophecy, and you should yield to the Spirit and speak in tongues. As you practice yielding, you will begin to speak out according to what the Spirit is saying. The Holy Spirit wants to speak the truth and start to correct things that are in this earthly realm. Out of your mouth will come God's thoughts toward you and His plans for your future. Your future will become your now. You will not worry about your circumstances anymore, because the Spirit is speaking the truth and correcting your course. Your future is in the hands of God, but God can show you things that are to come through His Spirit. This transaction is praying in the Spirit and allowing your physical voice to bring forth what is in the spirit, into this natural realm. The Spirit of God is the very breath of the Almighty.

The Spirit of God was the One who formed your spirit initially and then recreated it at the born-again experience. The Spirit of God has the ability to influence your body and your soul as well. This influence comes by you yielding your physical members and yielding your mind to the will of God. Without your body, you cannot live on this earth. You need your body, but you need to discipline it. You need to let the Spirit of God correct and cause you to walk in the power of God and not in the power of the flesh.

Your mind, will, and emotions need to be transformed with the help of the Holy Spirit who is dwelling inside of your spirit. You need to transform your mind, and you need to cause your mind, your will, and your emotions to be renewed by the Word of God and line up to God's will.

> *Do not be conformed to this world, but be transformed by the renewing of your mind, that you may prove what is that good and acceptable and perfect will of God.*
>
> —ROMANS 12:2

God could breathe on you right now and change everything about you. God does have breath, and it is a spiritual breath. Jesus Himself showed that His breath was the Spirit of God and that the Spirit of God causes people to be born-again in the Spirit.

Jesus showed that when you yield to the Spirit, you can prophesy. The apostle Paul explained that you can prophesy and speak forth mysteries in the Spirit by the gift of speaking in tongues. You can also manifest it in your own intelligible language when you speak forth the mysteries of God in understanding.

Paul said that you should pray for the interpretation of your tongues so that you can understand what you are saying. When you yield to the Spirit, there is prophecy; you speak forth in an intelligible language that you know. Sometimes you can speak in tongues, which can be an intelligible, earthly language, but it may not be one known by you. You are speaking mysteries unless someone understands what you are saying and can interpret your tongues or you have prayed to interpret them yourself.

God can speak through you by causing your spirit to be ignited in the other realm. Then, you manifest the voice of God through your lips and your tongue, and this happens in prayer all the time. You will be praying in the Spirit and something will come out in English, and you will learn to yield and interpret your tongues. You will then be able to understand what the Spirit is saying as this happens to me often. After a while, you get accustomed to interpreting what you are praying in tongues and what the Spirit of God is saying. You can yield to the Spirit, and you do not have to yield to the desires of the flesh.

BE A PART OF WHAT GOD IS DOING

It is the same thing with your mind. You need to renew your mind or re-educate your mind to respond according to the Word of God. Once you do that, all the limitations are off because it is your mind that limits you. Your body is fallen, and you only live a certain amount of years before you pass away. You understand those limitations are put on you, but there are a lot of other limitations placed on you mentally that you may not recognize. If you would allow the Holy Spirit through the Word of God to educate you, then you also would see those limitations taken off of you.

A limitation that you may encounter in your mind is that you may not think that God is speaking to you. You may not think that God cares about you, and you may have doubts and fears. That is why you need to be listening to the teachings of the Word of God. You always need to be renewing your mind by meditating on the Scriptures. God's Word causes your spirit and your mind to become part of what God is doing instead of your mind resisting what the Spirit is doing.

A STORY

We need to let the breath of God blow on us in order to encounter times of refreshing from Heaven. Sometimes, you will experience your heavenly Father and it is beyond words. I have spent time in the presence of God to where I have had revelation supernaturally flow over me like a river. There was a period of several weeks where this encounter continually happened, and I have never been the same. I have received such supernatural revelation that books were birthed and written in a very short period of time. One particular time, the power of the breath of God was so strong that I experienced healing in my body. God can breathe on you and things will change for the better.

Revelation and healing will flow in these last days as God breathes on us. We will hear God's voice like never before!

Chapter 8

HEARING GOD IN YOUR INNER MAN

If then you were raised with Christ, seek those things which are above, where Christ is, sitting at the right hand of God. Set your mind on things above, not on things on the earth.

—COLOSSIANS 3:1-2

THE APOSTLE PAUL WAS CAUGHT UP IN THE SPIRIT AND SAW and heard things that are beyond our comprehension. He shared some of those things with us in his letters to the churches. What is great about Paul is that he does not come right out and say how he learned all the spiritual things he wrote about. So every time he says something, you gather he learned the truth while he was caught up to be with the Lord. This man understood the behind the scenes, intricate workings of the Spirit of God.

Paul wrote to the Colossians, and he said if you were raised with Christ, seek those things which are above where Christ is seated at the right hand of God. You should set your mind on things above and not on things of the earth. I had this experience myself when I was in the heavenly realm before being sent back to earth. I did not want to come back. What was very apparent about living in this physical realm was that it is very hard to focus on spiritual things. Yet, you must focus on things above in the heavenly realm.

You can almost feel trapped down here in this physical realm. Everything here on earth looks and feels so real, but many things are lying signs and wonders. Many things you encounter here on earth are facts, but they are not truth. Absolute truth belongs in Heaven with the Holy Spirit. The Holy Spirit was sent to lead you into all truth, so He can speak contrary to the facts. For example, He can say, "You are healed," even though you have a disease and show all the symptoms. When the Lord says you are healed, you have to believe God and not your symptoms. Facts can be lies on this earth even though some people think that facts are truth. God's truth is absolute in Heaven, established at the throne of God. As Paul is saying, do not focus on things down here on the earth. Instead, focus on things above where Christ is seated at the right hand of God.

For he raised us from the dead along with Christ
and seated us with him in the heavenly realms
because we are united with Christ Jesus.
—EPHESIANS 2:6 NLT

This Scripture says that you were raised with Christ and seated with Jesus in the heavenly realms, and Paul is saying you are to set your mind there also. You are not to set your mind on things where you are in the physical realm but on Christ in the spiritual realm. That seems easy for Paul to say, but how do you do that?

DISCERNING TRUTH IN YOUR INNER MAN

A lot of people want to hear God's voice, but they set their minds on their passions and emotions. Everything about them is focused on the lower physical realm, and because of that, the voices of this earth are going to be louder than God's voice. That is not the way it should be for a Christian, but unfortunately, that is the case for many believers.

You can talk to people everywhere, and they want to hear God's voice, but they do not want to turn off the voice of this world. God is speaking just as loudly as those other voices, but they cannot hear Him. I have heard God's voice so loud that it shook everything, including the house, but other people there did not hear it. I do not understand how that works, but God opened my ears, and it felt to me like God was speaking to me audibly.

> *And no wonder! For Satan himself transforms himself into an angel of light.*
> —2 CORINTHIANS 11:14

If you are not focused on spiritual things and truth but only focused on facts, then Satan can come in and deceive you. Here,

Paul is saying that Satan can transform himself into an angel of light. He can look like an angel of God, and evil spirits that are familiar with you can move in and make it look like God is trying to say something to you. These evil spirits can manipulate your circumstances and take you in a certain direction that God does not want you to go in. These familiar spirits can follow your family and your relatives around for a very long time. They are very familiar with you and your family, and they can enforce curses and pass them down in your family for generations.

Evil spirits will always exist because they live forever, and they will not just disappear. Spiritual things do not just disappear. These evil entities will follow you around and try to speak to you and interject into your life. They will try to sound like God to deceive you into listening to them. Even Satan will act as an angel of light to try to lead you, but it is a deception. These spirits have an ability to deceive, so it is very important to understand in your heart or spirit that you are born again. When you know the truth, it sets you free. You are not led by circumstances anymore because you are led by the Spirit of God.

> *And you shall know the truth, and the truth shall make you free.*
>
> —JOHN 8:32

Your discernment needs to increase, and the reason I am telling you this is that I do not want you to be deceived. When I was in Heaven, I saw that there was such deception here on earth. If you are not careful, you could be drawn away by ungodly voices. You could be drawn away by familiar spirits that make it look like God is trying to tell you something, but it is actually evil spirits. I did not want to come back to the earth because I saw how deceptive it could be here; it is a war. Yet the Lord Jesus asked me to come back, and I am glad that I did. I am so glad that I can help people understand that you can hear God's voice, but it is in the places of the heart or inner man that you hear it.

> *And these signs will follow those who believe: In My name they will cast out demons; they will speak with new tongues; they will take up serpents; and if they drink anything deadly, it will by no means hurt them; they will lay hands on the sick, and they will recover.*
>
> —MARK 16:17-18

These signs that are talked about here in the Gospel of Mark are outward signs that manifest when believers are preaching the Word of God. These signs will inevitably follow those who believe, but there is a process. As a Christian, you do not seek after signs, but you preach the gospel and the Word of God. You speak the Word of God, and these manifestations from Heaven come automatically. God does the signs and the wonders, and you do the believing, the preaching, and the teaching. It is up to you to be the believer who will allow the manifestation of the Holy Spirit to come through you; and as you do your part, God will do His part.

In your walk with the Holy Spirit, you should see your intimacy with Him increasing. You also should see maturity increasing in your life because the Holy Spirit wants to increase your faith and your belief system. He wants you to be knowledgeable about what God loves and what He does not like. You are supposed to know these things and know God's ways. The Holy Spirit wants to increase your belief and increase your faith to the point where signs and wonders follow you. God will do His part if you do your part.

God wants you to speak into this earthly realm from the inner man by the power of the Holy Spirit. When you speak, you are to speak forth what God says—the will and the Word of God. The Spirit of God is giving you words to speak, and you are to speak them out with an audible voice. When you speak out the Word of God, you do that from the dwelling place, which is the secret place of the Most High God. What you speak comes out from your inner man into your environment, so then the environment around you encounters what the secret place inside of you is encountering.

If people are listening to the words you speak, they can attach themselves to that word and frequency that is from your inner man. When people attach themselves to what you say, they put faith in what you are saying, and faith is of the heart. You can tune into what God is doing through words and attach yourself to them. Suddenly, you start to experience the very place people in the spirit are speaking from.

If you are speaking by the Spirit of God, you can bring the whole room of people into that realm with you. It happens all the time in my meetings because I speak from the other realm. When that heavenly realm comes into the physical room, everyone in the meeting encounters it. Even watching videos of these meetings, you will encounter the other realm because I am yielding to the Holy Spirit. In that spiritual realm, there are many angels and flames of fire, and there is the power of the Holy Spirit. The anointing of God is all around me as I am speaking to you, and the anointing of God is coming out of me and into you.

You learn how to yield to the Spirit of God and speak from that place. Then God starts to manifest outwardly what is inward. You have to be a good receiver from Heaven. You have to be able to encounter that other realm and impart it to other people. God has already set it up for you to receive from Him. You can hear God's voice, and He wants to speak to you.

LIVING WATER WITHIN

When God speaks to you, He will deposit something in you by what He speaks, and that is an encounter every Christian must have. To have something from God to give out, you must receive something. God has already set it up through the born-again experience for you to receive communication from Him in the inner man. That is the deepest part of you where the Spirit of God dwells. It is through the amazing power of the Holy Spirit inside of you that God is speaking within you.

If you are born-again and baptized in the Holy Spirit, then God has already anointed you. He has caused you to flow with that great river of living water that flows up into eternal life from within you, inside of your spirit. There is no need for you to look for outward signs anymore because they will come. Signs will come because you are being led by the Holy Spirit and speaking the Word of God. You are bringing forth what God is saying from the other realm, and you believe it. Once that happens, signs and wonders will follow you.

> *But seek first the Kingdom of God and His righteousness, and all these things shall be added to you.*
>
> —MATTHEW 6:33

God says to seek Him and the Kingdom first, and He will supply all your needs (see Matthew 6:33). You will get to the place where everything that you want is added to you because you do not focus on it. You do not even have to pray for yourself or your needs because God is taking care of you. At this point, you can pray for others, interceding for them, and asking God to intervene in their lives. You need to let the Holy Spirit talk and pray through you for other people. The power of the Holy Spirit wants to fulfill what Paul referred to as the uniting of the body of Christ (see Ephesians 4:1-6). You are to build up the body, uniting it, and working with the Holy Spirit to help each one fulfill the plan of God in this dispensation through the church; it is all about other people.

When I was in Heaven, Jesus told me that I could come back to earth and it would all be extra credit. I told Him that I did not want to come back because of the warfare I saw taking place down here. My eyes were opened, and I did not want to come back because I saw that it is hard to live down here. Then Jesus taught and showed me the secrets of how to live down here successfully, and He showed me that I could win. The tools that He gave me I brought back with me, and it has really helped me and others. I have found since I came back that I have been more victorious and more mature than ever before.

Jesus said to me, "Kevin, you are not being sent back for yourself. Your returning is not about you. It is about the people who need to hear what you are going to tell them. People's lives will be rerouted and changed because you go back."

If you want to move with the Spirit of God, He is already moving, and you need to unite with Him. However, know that He will want to pray through you for other people. You will find that you won't need to pray for yourself as much. Not needing to pray for yourself was a key that I saw when I was on the other side. The Holy Spirit wants to talk to you, but He also wants to talk through you. Part of the desire of the Spirit is to get you to the place where you are victorious, so you can transfer that victory to others.

When you stop focusing on yourself, you will start to encounter angelic visitations. God's heavenly angels will come to help you minister to other people. Angels will join forces with you in what they are doing, and they will be ministering to people. You will be working with angels and ministering to others, and this unleashes a whole other realm of angelic visitation in your life. Angelic visitation is what started to happen to me when I stopped focusing on myself.

DISTRIBUTING THE KINGDOM

Then Jesus said to His disciples, "If anyone desires to come after Me, let him deny himself, and take up his cross, and follow Me. For whoever desires to save his life will lose it, but whoever loses his life for My sake will find it."

—MATTHEW 16:24-25

I know that some people do not want to hear this, but denying yourself is a very vital and major part of Christianity. You must deny yourself, pick up your cross, and follow Jesus and the crucified life. Part of denying yourself will cause all things that you need and want to be added to you because you sought after the Kingdom of God first. Angelic visitation will begin to occur in a great and mighty way in your life.

The power of the Holy Spirit is always ready, and the move of God is always happening. Our inability to discern what God is doing is because we focus on ourselves a lot. I am telling you what I saw on the other side, and I am not saying that I am perfect in this. I always remind myself of what I saw. You have to release yourself from the way religion has taught you and allow God to unhook you from the worldly system. God is telling you to go forth. He is telling you to preach, teach, and speak, and do not wait any longer.

The only time Jesus told the people of God to wait was for what they were to encounter on the Day of Pentecost when they received the Holy Spirit and were sent out. The Holy Spirit has been poured out, so there is no reason to wait for the Holy Spirit any longer. It is your responsibility to receive and learn how to yield your members to the Holy Spirit. The Spirit wants to take over your life, and He wants to own you and have every part of you.

God is speaking to you about the way He wants to move, and it is happening right now. Somewhere in your inner man, there is the voice of God talking to you right now. You are learning how to yield to it. Once you get to this place where you focus on God and others, then the Holy Spirit will start to use you. God will speak through you and help you be a distributor of what He is doing in the earth. The Kingdom of God is being distributed, and it is advancing. It is coming through the body of Christ, and it is coming through you.

Remember that flesh is flesh, and it will do what flesh does. But spirit will do what spirit does, and it is Spirit to spirit. *"It is the Spirit who gives life; the flesh profits nothing. The words that I speak to you are spirit, and they are life"* (John 6:63). Jesus said this! You must understand that the communication that goes on in your inner man is God speaking to you, Spirit to spirit, and it is life to you.

> *But I discipline my body and bring it into subjection, lest, when I have preached to others, I myself should become disqualified.*
> —1 CORINTHIANS 9:27

We have talked about renewing your mind, which involves getting your mind to stay on godly things and being seated with Christ in the heavenly realms. Now you have to think about your body as well. You not only have to renew your mind, but you also have to discipline your body. Paul said that he could be disqualified if he let his body rule and reign over him. If your body wants to do things that are wrong and you do not stop it, then your body could disqualify you from the race. Paul said that he disciplined his body daily.

> *For to me, to live is Christ, and to die is gain. But if I live on in the flesh, this will mean fruit from my labor; yet what I shall choose I cannot tell. For I am hard-pressed between the two, having a desire to depart and be with Christ, which is far better. Nevertheless to remain in the flesh is more needful for you. And being confident of this, I know that I shall remain and continue with you all for your progress and joy of faith.*
>
> —PHILIPPIANS 1:21-25

In this Scripture, Paul is talking about the voice of God and the deep places within our hearts. He is discussing how he wanted to go and be with the Lord while at the same time he wanted to stay on earth for the sake of others. Paul said that it would be far better for him to go, but because it would benefit others, he would stay. The gifts and callings of God that are without repentance were in Paul just like they are in you (see Romans 11:29). You want to fulfill everything that God has for you on this earth, and you want to fulfill the books written about you in Heaven. You know that God has good things written about you to accomplish, and angels are waiting to assist you to do it.

Paul knew that the things that were hidden in Christ were written, and part of that included Paul changing history. He was an apostle, but he probably did not know he would be used mightily for these past two thousand years. Paul's writings have changed the mindset of so many people. It was God's will that he stayed on the earth, spoke God's Word, and wrote even when he was in jail. Paul's revelation was transferred from generation to generation because he stayed on in the flesh. You will begin to live out your destiny in Christ, and it will change people's lives because you do your part.

The process all starts within you—in your inner man— and then it begins to come out from you. First, you must die to self so that the hidden man comes forth. The born-again spirit that is within you begins to live out of that revelation. The real you, your born-again spirit, then becomes unhindered. When you get revelation from the Word of God, you want to share it with somebody. When you share, it transfers that reality to another, which is what Paul did. What was revealed to Paul is now revealed to you. Accept it, believe it, listen to it, and adhere to it. Christians today are succeeding because of Paul's obedience and his success at doing what God asked him to do. Now you can be successful with what God is asking you to do.

Paul was very often incarcerated in jail under terrible circumstances. He only had a pen and parchment, and yet, because he yielded to what God had for him to do, he has inspired many generations in this world. He will forever be known as the apostle Paul. Stop looking outward for signs and start looking inward at the Spirit of God who dwells inside of you. Start focusing on things above where Christ is seated at the right hand of God; this is what God is asking you to do.

When you focus on things above, the voice of God will become stronger because the voice of God is in your spirit. On the earth, you must live out of your spirit even though you are in a body. The real you is on the inside, in the hidden places of your heart. You do not go by your circumstances; you go by what the Word of God says.

> *Therefore we do not lose heart. Even though our outward man is perishing, yet the inward man is being renewed day by day. For our light afflic-tion, which is but for a moment, is working for us a far more exceeding and eternal weight of glory, while we do not look at the things which are seen, but at the things which are not seen. For the things which are seen are temporary, but the things which are not seen are eternal.*
>
> —2 CORINTHIANS 4:16-18

Paul is sharing what he saw in Heaven. He says that you— the inward man—are being renewed and strengthened day by day while your body is deteriorating. Paul says that even though this is happening, it is just a light affliction because this life down here is not permanent. You have an exceeding great and eternal weight of glory working for you. You are not to see the things down here as being the absolute end of your faith. You are to see Christ seated at the right hand of God and those things which are eternal.

HEAVENLY HABITATION

> *For we know that if our earthly house, this tent, is destroyed, we have a building from God, a house*

not made with hands, eternal in the heavens. For in this we groan, earnestly desiring to be clothed with our habitation which is from heaven, if indeed, having been clothed, we shall not be found naked. For we who are in this tent groan, being burdened, not because we want to be unclothed, but further clothed, that mortality may be swallowed up by life. Now He who has prepared us for this very thing is God, who also has given us the Spirit as a guarantee. So we are always confident, knowing that while we are at home in the body we are absent from the Lord. For we walk by faith, not by sight. We are confident, yes, well pleased rather to be absent from the body and to be present with the Lord.

—2 Corinthians 5:1-8

Paul had this revelation of who you really are. You are a spirit who lives in a body that one day will go to the other side. One day, the real you will go on to Heaven, but until that time, you groan inside of yourself for the future. While you are in the body, this is your habitation down here, but your real true habitation is in Heaven where God has prepared a place for you to live. In Heaven, you will have a new body and live in a mansion.

Your body will be given back to you at the resurrection no matter how you died, where your body is or whether you were cremated or buried. It does not matter. God brings it all back together supernaturally, and you are given a wonderful, new, glorified resurrection body. *"For our dying bodies must be transformed into bodies that will never die; our mortal bodies must be transformed into immortal bodies"* (1 Corinthians 15:53 NLT).

I had the privilege to see and encounter that body in Heaven, and it was amazing. You are just visiting here while in this earth suit, your new glorified body and your real home are in Heaven.

I saw that I came back to this earth to be here for a certain amount of time to help people, and it benefits them because my reward has already been given to me in Heaven. I have been called faithful and was sent back to be a voice in this generation, and so it is with you. Your permanent home is in Heaven, and God has already destined this for you. He is working out all things for you, for it is His perfect will for your life. You do not need to worry about a thing because God is with you in a mighty way.

> *Yet in all these things we are more than conquerors through Him who loved us.*
> —ROMANS 8:37

You can go forth in the spirit of conquering because all that God has for you has been given to you through Jesus Christ. The limits have been taken off through Christ, and I know that you cannot fail because God has taken the limitations off.

> *There is therefore now no condemnation to those who are in Christ Jesus, who do not walk according to the flesh, but according to the Spirit.*
> —ROMANS 8:1

When you walk according to the Spirit, even your past is destroyed, so those limitations have also been taken off. You cannot look back because God has erased those things, and they are gone.

> *But if you indeed obey His voice and do all that*
> *I speak, then I will be an enemy to your enemies*
> *and an adversary to your adversaries.*
> —EXODUS 23:22

Not only is your past forgiven, but also the Lord is saying that if you will listen to Him and walk with Him, there are other limitations He will remove. God will be with you and come against your enemies to protect you because you are now His. God will go after your adversaries, and this is an amazing truth. When I was in Heaven, I saw that on this earth if you want to, you could engage God on a whole other level in the spirit.

KNOWN ACCORDING TO THE SPIRIT

> *Therefore, from now on, we regard no one accord-*
> *ing to the flesh. Even though we have known*
> *Christ according to the flesh, yet now we know*
> *Him thus no longer.*
> —2 CORINTHIANS 5:16

You are no longer to know anyone according to the flesh. God speaks to us Spirit to spirit, and you are to know everybody by the spirit now. The real you is the person God made you to be. Yield to the inner man where the Spirit of God dwells, and be encouraged that God is igniting you to do His perfect will. You need to be faithful, because every one of us needs you to be faithful and unite in these last days. Jesus told me to train people to walk in this so that everyone begins walking in the power of the Holy Spirit, and I work myself out of a job because so many others are doing the same ministry.

A STORY

While I was in my career for 29 years with a major airline, I would often watch Christian television with my wife when I got home from flying. I remember watching Jesse Duplantis as we would eat dinner. Because I was constantly praying in the Spirit all day quietly and meditating on the Word of God, I would say things without thinking them. Then, those things I would say would come to pass because I had actually yielded to the spirit of prophecy.

On one particular occasion, I turned to my wife as we were watching Jesse Duplantis preach on television and proclaimed, "One day I will write a book about my experience in Heaven with Jesus, and I will be on TBN. When I am, I want that man (Jesse Duplantis) to interview me."

Well, I had never met Jesse before, but three years after I said that, I met Jesse and his wife, Cathy. We were invited to lunch with them, and then the Lord told them to come bless our new house. We had just moved to Louisiana and bought a house in the same area as the Duplantis'. Later, Jesse and Cathy let us know that they were willing to ordain us. As Jesse laid hands on us during the ordination service, he was told by the

Lord to call Jan Crouch and bring me to TBN to interview on their network.

The show went very well and when that show was seen by Sid Roth's staff, I was asked to have an interview with Sid. I knew that the show would do well as God did visit us on the set while filming. It was destiny for all of us. Just like me, you can follow your spirit, and God will move you into your destiny!

Chapter 9

Your Mind, Will, and Emotions

Now may the God of peace Himself sanctify you completely; and may your whole spirit, soul, and body be preserved blameless at the coming of our Lord Jesus Christ.

—1 Thessalonians 5:23

Paul talks about the fact that you have three parts to you: spirit, soul, and body. The spirit part of you is the part that is born-again and becomes a new creature in Christ. Your soul also has three parts which are your mind, will, and emotions. When I went to Heaven, I left my body on the operating table and looked back to see it lying lifeless on the table. I had not disconnected from who I was just because I lost my body. I was still Kevin. I still had feelings, thoughts, and emotions that I had while in my body on earth, but they were all redeemed. I still had emotions and reasoning capabilities because I noticed that I had no fear. I could move around the room because I had a spirit body even though I saw my physical body on the operating table.

I could remember certain things about myself, and I remembered and saw things that were on the earth, but yet, I was in the other realm at that point. The unredeemed part of my soul did not come with me when I found myself outside of my body. In some supernatural way, God instantly sanctified my mind, will, and emotions that came with my spirit. I was a spirit with a soul, but I was not in my body.

You must understand that sometimes God's voice is clouded or obscured in your spirit because your mind, will, and emotions get involved. Your soulish nature can clutter things up and cause what is in your spirit to be unclear. You have to understand that when it comes to hearing the voice of God, your mind, will, and emotions must come under subjection to your spirit and the Holy Spirit, otherwise hearing God will remain difficult for you. That's why I am going into more detail in this chapter regarding the soulish realm. Once you deal with the soulish realm in your life, hearing God will become much, much easier for you as you learn to yield the Spirit.

CONNECTING TO THE PERFECT WILL OF GOD

And do not be conformed to this world, but be transformed by the renewing of your mind, that you may prove what is that good and acceptable and perfect will of God.

—ROMANS 12:2

We all want to know the will of God for our lives. We do not just want the acceptable will, but we want to walk in the perfect will of God. To do that, we need to hear from God, and the apostle Paul gives us some very important instructions to help us. Paul said we cannot allow ourselves to be conformed to this world, but we must be separate. We cannot allow the world to form us into what it wants us to be. Even though God wants us to be separate from the world, there are people and systems in place that try to control us, so we find ourselves in a struggle. But Paul tells us to refuse being conformed to this world but be transformed by the renewing of our minds. We renew our minds by the Spirit of God, the Word of God, and the will of God.

When you renew your mind, it helps you to prove what is the acceptable and perfect will of God for your life. You might feel rejected by the world, but at the same time that you feel rejected, God has accepted you. God loves you. He has chosen you, and He causes you to triumph. God is saying you are more than a conqueror (see Romans 8:37). You renew your mind by using the filter of what God says about you. In other words, do not let yourself feel rejected because you know it is not true. Your emotions can lie to you, and your mind can build a case against you that is not true because it is not what God says about you.

When I was in Heaven with Jesus, I saw that there was a part of me that resisted God and was in rebellion; it had to do with my will and my emotions. I saw that things like this had to be dealt with if you want to hear God's voice loud and clear and know that you are in God's perfect will all the time. There is a part of you that is not redeemed, and I saw that when I went to the other side, there was a part of me that did not come with me. However, my will, thoughts, and emotions that were completely redeemed and submitted to God did come with me.

> *When I was a child, I spoke and thought and reasoned as child. But when I great up, I put away with childish things.*

Paul talked about the maturity of a Christian to the Corinthians, and he said that even spiritually you do not want to remain a child but become spiritually mature. Your soul will need to be developed to become mature so that your spirit can side with your whole being and not just your inner man. Your inner man or spirit is born-again and all set; it knows the will of God and hears God's voice. The problem is the unredeemed parts of your soul (mind, will, and emotions) obscure your spirit's ability to hear God's voice clearly.

While I was out of my body, I saw that my soul was wrapped around my spirit from my face down to my chest area, and it was influenced by the world. I saw that my spirit was born again, and it was influenced by the Kingdom of God. My spirit knew no defeat, and it did not doubt or fear. It knew God's perfect will, but my soul did not know all those things. The unbelief and fear came from my emotions and my reasoning capabilities. I realized how people, including myself, sabotage their daily lives by their thinking and emotions.

In meekness instructing those that oppose them-
selves; if God peradventure will give them
repentance to the acknowledging of the truth.
—2 TIMOTHY 2:25 KJV

Paul says that there are people who oppose themselves. You do not want to be like that; you do not want to oppose what God is doing in you. Jesus did not come to earth and oppose the Father, He went around doing good and healing everyone who was oppressed by the devil (see Acts 10:38). Jesus saw what the Father wanted Him to do, and He did it. He did not oppose God, and you should never oppose what God is doing in your life. When you feel separated from God, it has to do with your mind, will, and emotions. Your spirit has to fight through the soulish nature because your spirit wants to do God's will.

QUIETING YOUR SOUL

Why are you cast down, O my soul? And why are
you disquieted within me? Hope in God, for I shall
yet praise Him for the help of His countenance.
—PSALM 42:5

David told his soul to find hope in God when it was dis-quieted. David's spirit man was talking to his soul and telling his soul to be quiet and settle down as he encouraged himself in the Lord. Remember that you can encourage yourself in the Lord. When David faced the giant, he was speaking out of his spirit when he prophesied that Goliath was defying the armies of God. David could see that all the soldiers and even King Saul were hiding from Goliath and operating out of a spirit of fear. David said that he was going to feed Goliath to the birds that day, and he was prophesying because he was speaking from the spirit and not out of his emotions.

People today react out of their emotions and from their minds or their reasoning, and because of that, they are not engaged in the battle. They are not strong in battle like King David, and they are not confronting their giants. I saw that if I was going to be sent back from Heaven, I would have to encourage people to engage the enemy. You must be rough with the devil—not afraid to drive him out. You must stop living out of your soul realm.

I saw that most Christians live out of their souls and not out of their spirits at all. Even activities in the church which are supposed to be spiritual are coming from the soul. There is so much soul activity in the lives of believers that they do not discern when a manifestation is of the soul or of the Spirit.

What areas of your life are you being challenged in right now? God is truly helping you to understand yourself. You have your soul and spirit, and you do not want to oppose God. You do not want to oppose yourself because you are a Christian. You must connect with what God is doing in the spiritual realm, and educate your soul with the Word of God. That is how you mature. Paul has given you the secret to overcoming your soul by not opposing yourself.

For one who speaks in an unknown tongue does not speak to people but to God; for no one understands him or catches his meaning, but by the

Spirit he speaks mysteries [secret truths, hidden things].
>   —1 Corinthians 14:2 AMP

Paul said that when you pray in tongues, you are speaking mysteries or praying out secrets, and this transaction is from the spiritual realm into the physical world. Speaking in tongues will help you to overcome your soul because it fortifies, encourages, and empowers your spirit. Whatever it is you are doing in life, make sure you are praying in tongues to empower yourself in the spirit to overthrow what is not of God.

Paul is telling you that the Holy Spirit can override and bypass your soul when you speak in tongues. Your mind cannot participate because it is a spiritual transaction. However, your spirit knows what you are saying, even though it is speaking in a different language. When you pray in tongues, hidden things not obvious to your understanding but that God has already deposited in your spirit, will come forth. You do not understand what you are saying in tongues because your spirit is speaking with God and bypassing your soul. If you walk in the spirit and want to hear God's voice, remember God is a Spirit, so you must speak to Him spirit to Spirit.

Your soul—your mind, will, and emotions—will be overridden by what the Spirit is doing. When you use your lips to pray in tongues, you are bringing what is in the spiritual realm into this realm. When you ignite yourself by praying in tongues and your spirit is praying, there will come a point where there is an overthrow. God brings understanding up through your spirit into your mind, and you gain the understanding because you learn how to yield to the Holy Spirit.

> *Now may the God of peace Himself sanctify you completely; and may your whole spirit, soul, and body be preserved blameless at the coming of our Lord Jesus Christ. He who calls you is faithful, who also will do it.*
>
> —1 THESSALONIANS 5:23-24

Paul is speaking about the three parts of man and explains that the God of peace Himself will sanctify you. He names these three parts and says that the Spirit wants to sanctify them completely and set them apart. I believe, without a doubt, that what opposes you in this life are your mind, will, and emotions because the Holy Spirit has not been allowed to sanctify them or set them apart to redeem them. One of the most important things you can learn to do is yield to the Holy Spirit within you. Your spirit is redeemed and completely set apart, but there is work that needs to be done so that you do not oppose yourself.

THE DIVISION OF SOUL AND SPIRIT

> *For the word of God is living and active and full of power [making it operative, energizing, and effective]. It is sharper than any two-edged sword, penetrating as far as the division of the soul and spirit [the completeness of a person], and of both joints and marrow [the deepest parts of our*

*nature], exposing and judging the very thoughts
and intentions of the heart.*

—HEBREWS 4:12 AMP

The Word of God and the Spirit of God are your answers to discerning and dividing between what your soul and Spirit are saying to you. You may not understand that you have a voice also, and you can actually hear opposing things within yourself. For example, you have feelings that go with your voice. You may feel like something is true, but it could be a falsehood. You could be lied to and believe the lie, but all the while your spirit in the deepest part of you knows what you believe is not true. That is why in these last days, the Spirit of God has to come into your life in a stronger manner to energize your spirit or inner man. The Word of God divides and cuts and separates so that you can discern the thoughts and intents of your heart from your own thoughts and feelings. Yielding to the Spirit of God and the Word of God will cause you to become a mature Christian walking in the perfect will of God.

When I was in Heaven, Jesus told me that the number one way that you can participate in the supernatural and overcome this world is by praying in the Spirit (praying in tongues) continually. I know this is controversial to some people, but Paul prayed in tongues. The Bible never says to stop praying in tongues. Since the beginning of the Christian dispensation until now, nothing has changed, and it is not over yet. The things of this age of the church have not ceased and are still in operation.

The Spirit of God supernaturally wants to pray a heavenly language through you. You need to yield to the Holy Spirit and allow your discernment to go to a higher level. I talk to people all the time, and many things they believe are incorrect. There are a lot of people who do not want to be deceived. One reason for wrong belief is a lack of understanding of God's Word. God's Word sharpens what you believe, and then the Spirit of God sides with the Word of God and manifests in power in your life.

When you pray in the Spirit, you are building up your spiritual life, and your inner man gets stronger and stronger. Then one day, an overthrow happens in your inner man. When it happens, it is Satan who becomes the victim instead of you. You are no longer a victim when your mind, will, and emotions are no longer allowed to have a loud voice in your life anymore. Your mind, will, and emotions have worked against you, but they are not allowed to vote against you anymore. So many people I have met are moving in the wrong direction because they are opposing themselves.

To build up your spiritual life so you don't oppose yourself, you need to meditate on the Word of God. I recommend that you begin with ten minutes a day meditating on a small portion of Scripture. Along with this, you must pray in the Spirit, beginning with ten minutes a day. After a while, you should begin to build up from there, meditating longer as you grow more mature. Then build up yourself to where you can pray for at least one hour a day. This is how you build up yourself in the knowledge of God and renew your mind, will, and emotions.

When you pray in the Spirit, you are praying in the power of God. You are building up yourself in your most holy faith and staying in the love of God (see Jude 1:20). These two things we've talked about—meditating in the Word for ten minutes and praying in tongues for ten minutes—will help you grow and mature exponentially. Make a plan to begin with these twenty minutes each day and, eventually, add ten minutes on to it to pray for others. If you do this, you will see such a turnaround in your life. I cannot wait to see what the Lord does through you.

The spirit is willing, and the flesh is weak (see Matthew 26:41). Remember that the power that raised Jesus from the dead is dwelling in you (see Romans 8:11), and that power is in your spirit. Your soul—your mind, will, and emotions—will need to be turned and changed. But there is an overthrow that will happen. Your spirit will get so strong it stands up and boldly starts to speak. That is when your soul has to step back and be submissive, and that is what you want. You need to pray in the Spirit, meditate on the Word of God, and not let your mind or emotions bother you; this takes discipline. Then you will be hearing God's voice and submitting to the perfect will of God for your life.

A STORY

When you pray in the Spirit, your inner man or human spirit will be ignited and built up (see Jude 20). This will cause you to discern that part of you. As you meditate on the Word of God, that process will cause a division between your soul and your spirit, and you will be able to discern more accurately the will of God. I found that the author of Hebrews can be a great help in hearing God's voice. Listen to what he says: *"For the word of God is alive and powerful. It is sharper than the sharpest two-edged sword, cutting between soul and spirit, between joint and marrow. It exposes our innermost thoughts and desires"* (Hebrews 4:12 NLT).

When I am thinking about entering into a relationship with someone, the Holy Spirit will help me understand God's will for the situation. For instance, when I was dating, I felt that I was supposed to wait for the right person. I was continually discerning in my heart as a relationship progressed as to whether the person was the one I was to marry. Finally, I was led by the Spirit of God to my wife, and we were married in a short amount of time. I was glad I waited, and we have been married now for over 27 years at the time of this book being published.

Make sure to let your spiritual life develop by the reading of the Word of God and praying in the Spirit. This will make such a difference when you need to hear the voice of God in a particular situation.

Chapter 10

PRAYING IN THE SPIRIT

And they were all filled with the Holy Spirit
and began to speak with other tongues,
as the Spirit gave them utterance.
—ACTS 2:4

THE HOLY SPIRIT CAME TO EARTH ON THE DAY OF
Pentecost. Jesus told His followers to wait for that day when the
Comforter and Helper would come to be with them forever.
The Holy Spirit came, and when He introduced Himself to the
people, several interesting manifestations occurred. He came in
with a mighty rushing wind. He came with tongues of fire over
the people's heads, and He came with utterance.

Jesus' followers started to speak in other languages that they
did not know, and they all became drunk in the Spirit. They
looked like they were drunk even though it was the middle of
the day. Peter had to get up to apologize and tell the multitude

outside that they were not drunk as they supposed, but this was what was spoken by the prophet Joel. *"And it shall come to pass afterward that I will pour out My Spirit on all flesh..."* (Joel 2:28).

> *For if I pray in a tongue, my spirit prays, but my mind is unproductive [because it does not understand what my spirit is praying]. Then what am I to do? I will pray with the spirit [by the Holy Spirit that is within me] and I will pray with the mind [using words I understand]; I will sing with the spirit [by the Holy Spirit that is within me] and I will sing with the mind [using words I understand].*
>
> —1 CORINTHIANS 14:14-15 AMP

Speaking in tongues is a weapon and a spiritual exercise that God gives you. Paul explained that when you pray in an unknown tongue, your spirit prays, but your mind does not participate because it does not have any understanding of it. Your body and your mind are outside of this experience because they cannot participate in this spiritual exercise. When you are born again, only your spirit is redeemed through the blood of Jesus. Your soul and your body are not redeemed. The Holy Spirit makes all things new in your *spirit*, but your mind still needs to be renewed, and your body still needs to be disciplined by you.

Unfortunately, because your mind and your body do not participate when you pray in tongues, they will do everything they can to pull you out of this spiritual exercise. That is why you need to renew your mind by the Word of God and discipline your body. Freedom comes into your spirit when the Holy

Spirit comes. *"For the Lord is the Spirit, and wherever the Spirit of the Lord is, there is freedom"* (2 Corinthians 3:17 NLT).

In First Corinthians, Paul differentiates between praying in tongues, which you *do not* understand, and praying in your known language, which you *do* understand. Paul says that you can do both, and I have found that I can operate in both realms—the spirit and the mind. I can pray in tongues and not have the understanding, but then I pray for the understanding and it comes forth. When you pray in the Spirit, you should pray that you can interpret what you are saying. Ask God to help you understand what the Spirit is praying through you, and He will do it.

When I pray in tongues, I look down into my spirit and not up into my head. I look to see if some part of the understanding of what I prayed in tongues is coming up from the Spirit. The Holy Spirit can give you understanding and give you the interpretation of what you are saying. However, when you pray in the Spirit, and you do *not* interpret, then only your spirit is edified. Your understanding does not comprehend, so your understanding is *not* edified.

Jude said to build yourself up in your most holy faith by praying in the Holy Spirit. He also said to keep yourself in the love of God and to look for the mercy of our Lord Jesus Christ unto eternal life. The love of God and His mercy cause me to want to know what God is saying to me. When I pray in tongues, I know that my mind isn't going to understand everything, but I take time to ask the Holy Spirit to show me, and perhaps, give me a glimpse of something the Holy Spirit is saying to me.

On the last day, that great day of the feast, Jesus stood and cried out, saying, "If anyone thirsts, let him come to Me and drink. He who believes in Me, as the Scripture has said, out of his heart will flow rivers of living water." But this He spoke concerning the Spirit, whom those believing in Him would receive; for the Holy Spirit was not yet given, because Jesus was not yet glorified.

—JOHN 7:37-39

I want to share what to meditate on and show you what to do to hear God's voice in a greater way. It is important to meditate on Scriptures that speak about hearing from God. If I am able, I meditate on a Scripture every day. When I meditate on the Scripture above, I break it down first. For example, I begin to think of Jesus is referring to the Holy Spirit as the river of living water. So I think of the Holy Spirit inside of me as a river of life. I think about how that means there is no death involved—just pure life inside of me.

John says that the Spirit of God will well up within you and flow out of you when you pray in tongues. The Spirit of God comes up into your mouth, onto your tongue and causes you to form words. It is important to note that these words will not come from your mind because your mind does not comprehend them. They will come up by the Spirit. The words will form in your mouth, and you will speak them out. As you pray in tongues and speak by the Spirit, the life of God will spring forth out of you. As Jesus said here, "Out of your heart will flow rivers of living water."

The Holy Spirit will even speak out about your future when you are praying. I actually had someone who was practically a stranger to me understand what I was saying in tongues because I was speaking his native language. He interpreted names and places of future events. Within a day, these things that the Holy Spirit spoke through me started to happen. This young man and I had just met. There was no way he could know these specific things about me, but they all came to pass. The Spirit was speaking my future, and I just thought I was praying in tongues. These are just a few of the things that have happened to me and the experiences I have had with the Holy Spirit confirming the Scriptures to me.

The holy fire of God that is coming forth out of your spirit is changing people's lives all around you, and you need to yield to that fire. Let that fire come out of you to change people's lives. Praying in tongues is also praying from the fire, and you can pray from the fire of the altar of God. The Lord wants to help you by igniting you and igniting your words through holy fire. People need to hear the pure unadulterated Word of God, which is incorruptible seed (see 1 Peter 1:23). If you are praying by the Spirit, which is the Holy Spirit, that is God's voice, and God is speaking through you.

I would pray for hours and hours a day, and then be able to hear God's voice a lot clearer. There were still times when I did not hear His voice because of warfare I was encountering. As a general rule, if you pray in tongues often and have times of being quiet, you *will* start to hear the Lord leading and guiding you in the direction He wants you to go.

CONFRONTING DEVILS AND GIANTS

And Jesus said to them, "I am the bread of life. He who comes to Me shall never hunger, and he who believes in Me shall never thirst.

—JOHN 6:35

If you eat God's Word every day and pray in tongues every day, then it begins to merge inside of you. That divine connection between God and you will cause you to have holy fire, and from out of that fire, you speak the Word of God by the power of the Holy Spirit. This connection reinforces the relationship that you have in your inner man with God because in your spirit you are one with the Holy Spirit. The Word becomes engrafted in you and becomes part of your being.

As you pray in tongues, meditate on the Word of God, and then speak the Word out, you will begin to see the synchronization of Heaven coming forth. If you do this every day, you will grow into a spiritual giant, and it will not take long. You have to be consistent, meditating every day. Just as you would go and work out at the gym to stay fit, you must consistently sow into your spiritual life.

The Word of God becomes part of you in your spirit, and it becomes ignited. Your soul is no longer able to influence your spirit, and your mind, will, and emotions become submitted to your spirit. After a while, your emotions and your mind submit to the will of God. When I was in Heaven, I saw that speaking in tongues is one of the most important things that you can do when you are on the earth. This particular subject, praying in tongues, was essentially one of the reasons I was sent back to earth. *It is the number one way of participating and being a partaker of the supernatural realm of God.*

When you are praying in tongues, your body sees that it can no longer influence your spirit, and it has to submit and back out. You will learn to rule and reign over your mind and your body because your spirit gets strong from praying in tongues and meditating on the Word of God. When you consistently apply these spiritual exercises, then your walk with God becomes easier. You will no longer have the troubles that you once had, and your dominion will increase in your realm and the realm around you.

You live in such an exciting time because never before has revelation been as strong as it is now in this day. People all over the world are going to start walking in the power of God like never before. Discernment and the power of the resurrection is coming to the body of Christ. People are starting to see that they are truly sons and daughters of God. They are seeing the need to submit to the Spirit, the need to pray in the Spirit, and the need to walk in the power of God. There is a tremendous need to walk out the crucified life. This is all going to happen. In fact, it is starting to happen right now.

You must be forceful with the devil. You need to confront devils and their evil works. You need to do this for yourself, and you need to do it for others. You must become strong. A lot of times, I see that Christians are not rough enough with the devil, and because of that, demons do not always leave like they are supposed to. You have to be rough with them and convince them that you *know* what authority you are walking in.

I do what King David did when he came after the giant Goliath. David told Goliath what he was going to do to him and told him that he was defying the armies of the living God (see 1 Samuel 17:26). David was not afraid of that giant, and I want to be like David. I want to build my spirit up to the point where there is an overthrow of my soul, just like when David told Goliath that he was going to die that day. The devil is the god of this world, and he has been defeated by Jesus Christ. You have been given authority and the name of Jesus, and at that name, every knee will bow and every tongue will confess that Jesus Christ is Lord (Philippians 2:10-11).

The power of God wants to influence your spirit so that your spirit can, in turn, influence your soul. When God comes into your life, He influences your spirit, and He causes you to be born again. The Holy Spirit ignites a fire from inside of you, and then your spirit begins to influence your soul. Your spirit tells your soul what is wrong and begins to correct to your soul. When you influence yourself with the Word of God and pray in tongues, it fortifies your spirit and builds you up spiritually. Your spirit will begin to overthrow your soul and prevent you from opposing yourself any longer; God does not want your spirit and your soul to fight each other.

As a Christian, your spirit is already born again, and your mind is being renewed and transformed by the Word of God. You cannot get any more saved than you are now. The born-again experience, through the blood of Jesus, takes care of everything. Your past is forgiven, and you are now a new creature, everything that was old is passed away and all things have become new (see 2 Corinthians 5:17).

OVERTHROWING THE SOUL REALM

You will not be any more holy than you are right now, and you will not be more righteous than you are now positionally in Christ Jesus. The blood of Jesus has cleansed you of all your sin, and the condition of sin has been taken away. Now you must walk out your life by faith. Every day you need to operate in repentance and confession for the things that happen daily in your life. You need to walk in the fear of the Lord with a sober mind, an appreciative heart, and a humble spirit. Your soul needs to be renewed, and you do that by the Word of God. Tell your mind the truth that is in God's Word.

I always tell my soul that I am a victor, and I am not a victim. I always overthrow my soul and tell it when it is wrong. If there is a conflict within me, I measure it by what is in my spirit and what is in the Word of God. I always come against my soul and my body when they act up, and that is how I discipline them.

The devil will try to talk to you in your mind or body. He will try to convince you or influence you in your emotions in some way. If you fortify yourself by renewing your mind, then it is harder for him to convince you because your spirit is already saved. When you believe in Jesus Christ and confess your sins and repent, then the overthrow of your *spirit* happens at that moment. By the power of the Holy Spirit, you are saved. However, it is up to *you* to cause the overthrow to happen in your soul by convincing your soul when it is wrong and must change.

When the devil comes to harass you, you need to address him and his lies and remind him that he is defeated. Never listen to him, and do not consider the things he is saying to you. When Eve was in the garden, she should not have considered the devil's lies because she already knew the truth. God came and spoke with her every day in the garden. Eve did not need to talk to an animal about theology. She needed to wait for God to come down and talk about these things, but she did not do that. Adam and Eve were deceived, and that is why we live in a fallen world and why Jesus had to come back and redeem us.

From the beginning, God always wanted to have communication and fellowship with us. Jesus disarmed the devil and the rulers, the authorities, and the supernatural forces that are operating around us. Jesus did this by triumphing over them through the cross, and He did this for us. He made a public example of those principalities and powers exhibiting them as captives in a triumphal procession, having triumphed over them through the cross (see Colossians 2:15 AMP). So tell the devil that he has already been defeated. There is no way he can win now. Begin now addressing the powers that exist right now around you and realize that Jesus has already given victory to you.

David said that God restored his soul. *"He restores my soul; He leads me in the paths of righteousness for His name's sake"* (Psalm 23:3). When you enter into God's rest, your soul can enter into that rest and be restored as well. There is a spiritual rest which translates over into your soul. You need to be balanced in all areas, physically, psychologically, and spiritually. You need to encounter God on all those different levels. The only way you can do that is through transference from the spiritual into the psychological and then into the physical. The need for this transference is something that is not being taught and needs to be corrected. I saw the need for it when I was in Heaven.

The Word of God in Heaven wants to correct and heal you and needs to be spoken to do that. There is healing coming to you, and it is a correction because you are not supposed to be sick. God never meant for people to be sick. He will cause you to walk supernaturally. Your spirit always will participate in the supernatural and remember that God's will for you is to be healed. That is a spiritual thing that needs to come into the physical realm.

Once you have built yourself up spiritually, there is a transference within you from the spiritual realm to your physical and psychological makeup. Meditate on the following points to support this process.

1. Your soul and your body need to be told what to do. They will not do it on their own. Accepting this fact will then help you deal with them appropriately.

2. Only your spirit knows what to do on its own because its guidance is set in the inner part of you by the Holy Spirit who dwells within you. The Spirit is inside of your spirit when you are born again, and Jesus said that the Holy Spirit would never leave you.

3. It is your body and your mind that need guidance and need to be told what to do. Sometimes you must speak firmly to your body and soul and say, "No, you are not going to do that. You

are going to do what God wants you to do." Addressing your body and soul is the one thing that most Christians do not understand, and it is most important.

4. Before you know it, your body and your soul will submit to your spirit man. Eventually, you will win, and the breakthrough will happen. Overthrow will happen when your spirit is built up enough through the Word of God and praying in tongues. Your soul and your body will want to submit, and they will finally give up, obey you, and submit to your spirit man. You will begin to do things that are led by your spirit and the Spirit of God, and then you will rule and reign by the Spirit. *"For as many as are led by the Spirit of God, these are sons of God"* (Romans 8:14). If you walk in the Spirit, you please God, but if you *do not* walk in the Spirit, you *cannot* please God (see Romans 8:8).

5. Right now, the demons are hoping you stay deceived; they want all people to be deceived, *especially* Christians. The devil does not want Christians moving into the inheritance and awesome power and authority they have through Jesus Christ. The devil does not want you to pray in tongues. The *one* thing that the devils fight more than anything else is the authority that you have through Jesus Christ. The demons actually quiver and shake to think that

you will learn to have command over them and come to know your authority and use it. They are very nervous right now that I am telling you this because they do not want to be overthrown. The devil has tried to keep you in a small place by keeping you in a victim mode, but you are breaking free right now!

6. *"And you shall know the truth, and the truth shall make you free"* (John 8:32). Christians are ordained by God to rule and reign on this earth. That is the way it is supposed to be, so your behavior has to be modified. Tell your body and your mind the way you are supposed to be acting. Then act like your Father God, being an imitator of Him (see Ephesians 5:1).

AGREEING WITH GOD

Jesus answered, "Most assuredly, I say to you, unless one is born of water and the Spirit, he cannot enter the Kingdom of God. That which is born of the flesh is flesh, and that which is born of the Spirit is spirit."

—JOHN 3:5-6

You have the Spirit of God inside of your spirit. He is ruling and reigning, and your soul is in submission to whatever God says. Everything that God says, your soul and your body must agree with it. Now, whatever it is that God is telling you, your spirit will agree with it, but your soul might fight it. You have to learn how not to oppose God in your mind, will, and emotions. You must not allow your body to take you away from the perfect will of God. I was sent back from Heaven by Jesus Himself to explain these things in great detail so that you can experience victory in your life.

> *Watch and pray, lest you enter into temptation.*
> *The spirit indeed is willing, but the flesh is weak.*
> —MATTHEW 26:41

When I was in Heaven, I got to see how things work down here on earth more clearly and what is going on behind the scenes. I was shown many ways that I could have overcome in my life. A part of me thought about how I could have done so much better and so much more in my life if I had known the fullness of these things and the reality of them. Jesus said that He could send me back, and I could change history and change a generation's way of thinking. And you know I agreed to do that, and I came back from the dead. These Scriptures in Galatians and Matthew are key Scriptures to help people live the crucified life and not give in to the flesh.

> *I have been crucified with Christ; it is no longer I*
> *who live, but Christ lives in me; and the life which*
> *I now live in the flesh I live by faith in the Son of*
> *God, who loved me and gave Himself for me.*
> —GALATIANS 2:20

Paul said that he had been crucified with Christ, which means it was no longer he who lived but Jesus' resurrection living inside of him. It was as though Jesus was borrowing Paul's body and living through him. You must realize that part of what short-circuits the power of God in your life is your flesh. It is your flesh getting in the way and preventing you from living the crucified life. Again, this is not a popular message today, but it will be.

A lot of people do not want to hear about denying themselves and doing what God wants them to do. They think that God loves them, so they should be allowed to do whatever they want. But that is not the case, and that is not the Jesus I met. From what I saw of the Kingdom in Heaven and what I saw of the Kingdom of God on the earth, it is more military like. Military in the sense that God has already established truth, and He is uncompromising about it. God does not want us to change the truths He has already established.

The verse in Matthew 26:41 is a key, and it is what Jesus said in the garden to His disciples. Jesus told them to pray so that they would not enter into temptation. His statement implies that temptation was available but had not been taken away. Jesus was telling the disciples that they were about to be tempted and to pray so they would not enter into it. It was so profound when Jesus said, *"The spirit is willing, but the flesh is weak."* He was saying, in other words, that they were fighting their flesh, and they had to pray they would not fall into temptation by the weakness of their flesh. It is important to remind yourself of this verse every day.

Jesus wanted the disciples to pray because He knew what was right ahead. Every day remind yourself that Jesus already knows what you are about to encounter. Every day you must listen to what is down in your spirit. Jesus will start to talk to you and tell you that something is coming up, and you need to begin to pray. When you yield to the Spirit of God and pray in tongues, you might be praying out something that has not happened yet. By the power of the Holy Spirit interceding in tongues, it could be resolved before it ever happens!

Jesus knew that His disciples were about to fall in the garden. That was why He said that the spirit is willing, but the flesh is weak. That is the way it should be with you. You should know that you are weak within yourself in the flesh, but you can pray in tongues and have victory over any circumstance. The Spirit of God wants to help you and pre-empt things in your life before they ever happen. The Spirit of God wants you to yield to Him as you pray and crucify the flesh. Do not let the flesh rule over you, but let the Spirit of God take over. Let Him coach you and help you in every way.

> *Then Jesus said to His disciples, "If anyone desires to come after Me, let him deny himself, and take up his cross, and follow Me."*
> —MATTHEW 16:24

Jesus' command is that if you desire Him and want to follow Him, you must deny yourself. You must say "no" to everything you want and say "yes" to Jesus. Then you take up the symbol of crucifixion, which is the cross, and follow Him. Jesus mandates that you must live the crucified life.

> *Or do you not know that he who is joined to a harlot is one body with her? For "the two," He*

> *says, "shall become one flesh." But he who is joined to the Lord is one spirit with Him. Flee sexual immorality. Every sin that a man does is outside the body, but he who commits sexual immorality sins against his own body. Or do you not know that your body is the temple of the Holy Spirit who is in you, whom you have from God, and you are not your own? For you were bought at a price; therefore glorify God in your body and in your spirit, which are God's.*
>
> —1 CORINTHIANS 6:16-20

When you are born again, you join yourself with the Spirit of God and become one with God. It would be best to meditate on this Scripture to help you understand the intimate relationship with the Lord Jesus Christ you have through the Spirit of God. Your spirit is joined to the Lord, and your body must listen to your spirit. Paul said to flee sexual sin because of the influence it will have on you. Your whole life has to be influenced by the Spirit and not by the world. You should not attach yourself to anything of the world. Spiritually you are joined to the Lord, and you should enjoy that union you have through the Holy Spirit.

UNITY WITH THE HOLY SPIRIT

> *As His divine power has given to us all things that pertain to life and godliness, through the knowledge of Him who called us by glory and virtue, by which have been given to us exceedingly great and*

precious promises, that through these you may be
partakers of the divine nature, having escaped the
corruption that is in the world through lust.

—2 PETER 1:3-4

Every time I read this Scripture, it still hits me so strongly. When I was in Heaven, I saw the way things are up there, and then I saw how it was meant to be down here on the earth. Even though I had passed on and was in Heaven with the Lord, Jesus let me look down and see how it really is here on earth. As I looked back at the earth, I saw that there was a discrepancy, a difference between what it *should* be like here and what is *actually* happening here. I saw that you were supposed to allow the glory of God that is inside of you as a Christian to come out. You were meant to become a partaker of that glory—the essence of spiritual life that Jesus Christ bought for you. God said that you could have part of His nature and be a partaker of it.

Man was created in the image of God, so he is a replica of God. He is not God, but he was close to the image of God (see Genesis 1:26). God does not have a body as we do, because He is a Spirit. God made us of flesh and blood, and He sent Jesus back to redeem us with a body of flesh and blood. God does not have the same flesh, bones, and blood that we have, but Jesus did. While Jesus was on the earth, He walked in victory, and He walked in the same power that we can walk in. Jesus said that what He had done on this earth, we also would do and that we would do even greater works (see John 14:12). The same Spirit that raised Jesus from the dead and brought Him to come back to life is the same Spirit inside of us.

But if the Spirit of Him who raised Jesus from the dead dwells in you, He who raised Christ from the dead will also give life to your mortal bodies through His Spirit who dwells in you.

—ROMANS 8:11

God's Spirit has quickened your mortal body and will not cause you to sin. There is nothing inside of your spirit that wants to sin because you are a new creature in Christ. When you yield to the Holy Spirit and pray in the Spirit, you are praying out of that divine nature. You are praying out of the same kind of nature that God has, and the same character that He has is inside of you. That is why it is so important to yield to the Spirit every day and to pray in the Spirit as much as possible.

God's Spirit inside of you will even quicken your mortal (physical) body. Praying in the Spirit will cause you to be in unity with the Holy Spirit, which will affect your physical body. You will begin to feel life and healing coming into your body and even your mind. Your mind will be renewed and corrected; it is a supernatural event. Your mind, will, and emotions will come into subjection to the will of God, and you will begin to rule and reign.

But we speak the wisdom of God in a mystery, the hidden wisdom which God ordained before the ages for our glory, which none of the rulers of this age knew; for had they known, they would not have crucified the Lord of glory. But as it is written: "Eye has not seen, nor ear heard, nor have entered into the heart of man the things which God has prepared for those who love Him." But

God has revealed them to us through His Spirit. For the Spirit searches all things, yes, the deep things of God.

—1 CORINTHIANS 2:7-10

The Holy Spirit in you is a Spirit of power and also a Spirit of revelation. The revelation of the Holy Spirit can access all the mysteries of God. The mysteries of God are in the heart of God, and He takes His heart and puts it into yours. Whatever God has in His heart right now is His intention for you, and He will put it into your spirit. The revelation of the Spirit is a communication between you and God happening all the time.

God has given you His heart so that you can know His intents. The Spirit will search all the deep things of God and make them known to you by His Spirit. You have to rely on the Holy Spirit and open up yourself to the movement of the Spirit. Living the crucified life is crucial for the Holy Spirit to be able to move in your life.

You have been called to a supernatural life in Christ Jesus, to participate and be a partaker of the divine nature. Remember God is a Spirit, and you were created as a spirit that lives in an earthly body. God is giving you what is of Him and placing it inside of you. You can have miracles happen in your life if you can capture all these truths and allow the impartation to be implemented into your life.

You must allow all the reasoning faculties over your mind and your will to be submitted to God. They are limiting you because they do not have the proper education of what the Word of God says. You cannot allow your body or your soul—your mind, will, and emotions—to limit you any longer. Adopt what Jesus and the Holy Spirit are saying inside of you; what Father God is communicating into your spirit by the Holy Spirit.

To hear God's voice, you must tell your body it will not talk you out of the will of God, and it will not say or do things that are not the will of God. You must tell your soul that will not speak against God's will but will be quiet and submissive to the will of God. Your body will sit in God's presence, and it will yield to the presence of God. When you yield, you will pray in tongues. When you pray in tongues, your spirit will pray out the perfect will of God and the mysteries of God.

In the spirit realm, there are many more dimensions than you have in the three-dimensional world in which you live. The Holy Spirit is willing to take you into other realms and other dimensions where you will experience freedom and liberty.

Your mind will limit you unless you get to work at transforming it by the Word of God. God is speaking to you by His Spirit right now inside of you. He is telling you the truth, and He is telling you that you can hear His voice. God wants to have wisdom placed inside of you, and He wants you to have a heart of passion to seek after Him. He wants you to pray in the Spirit as much as you can. He wants you to have the desires of your heart. God wants to close the gap between you and Him to the point where you can be one with Him. That was God's original intent for man and the way it is supposed to be. Jesus did all of this on the cross for you, but you must implement it into your life.

Chapter 11

GOD'S WORD WITHIN

*"If you're able to understand this, then you need
to respond." Then his disciples approached Jesus
and asked, "Why do you always speak to people
in these hard-to-understand parables?"*
—MATTHEW 13:9-10 TPT

I WANT TO SHARE WITH YOU SOME THINGS ABOUT JESUS'
personality that I became aware of when I was with Him. Jesus
knows much more than you will ever know, and no matter what
He shows you, there will always be more. As I was talking to Him,
He was showing me things constantly through revelation, and it
was just amazing. When you are asking Jesus for something or
asking the Holy Spirit to reveal things to you, ask them to show
the Word of God unto you so there will be a crop produced.

I ask for understanding all the time, and I always sow the
Word of God into me. The greatest thing about Jesus is that He

is the Word of God, the Bread of Heaven, and you can partake of Him like bread (see John 6:51). The most important thing you can do besides praying in the Spirit is sowing the Word of God into your heart and letting it produce a crop.

> *He explained, "You've been given the intimate experience of insight into the hidden truths and mysteries of the realm of heaven's kingdom, but they have not. For everyone who listens with an open heart will receive progressively more revelation until he has more than enough. But those who don't listen with an open, teachable heart, even the understanding that they think they have will be taken from them."*
> —MATTHEW 13:11-12 TPT

There is even more profound revelation as Jesus continues to teach. When you listen from an open heart, you will receive progressive revelation. If you have a teachable heart, more revelation will be given to you. I am always willing to hear what God is saying. I always want to be willing to change if something I am doing or believing is wrong. You must remain teachable and always willing to change. That is the way you have to be to receive God's revelation. I know you want to hear God's voice of revelation.

THE PARABLE OF THE SOILS

The Word of God is the voice of God, and it is a seed planted inside the garden of your heart. Jesus said there are four different soils, but only one of them produces a crop. You must discern the condition of the soil of your heart. You must discern what is going on with your soil so that the Word of God will have its way in your heart. Read Jesus' parable of the soils in Matthew 13 in the Passion Translation to prepare for this impartation.

The Hard Soil

The first type of soil Jesus speaks about is the hard soil. It is the soil that is on the beaten path and hardened by many people walking on it. When seed falls on hard soil, we hear the Word of God but walk away not understanding it. There is a lack of understanding and a hardness of heart, so the Word of God does not take root. The truth was not grasped or understood. Sometimes what we think we hear God say on the surface and what He really intends can be a whole different story.

I notice with Jesus that there are depths to what He says. There are intentions as to why He says what He says, and I want to know it all. I want to know Jesus' intentions, so I always ask the Lord to reiterate things and show me the truth. The beaten path and the hardened soil do not produce a crop because the evil one comes and takes it away before it can become rooted. If you have hardened soil, you do not understand or grasp the truth, and now the evil one comes and takes the seed away from you.

The mystery behind the Word of God is the intent of God, and that is what you need to grasp here. Some people you will minister to are hard-hearted, and that is the condition of their heart. They will hear the Word of God, but they do not take it into their hearts and do not grasp its intent. In order to minister to these people and get them to soften up their hearts, it requires the healing power of God.

At the beginning of my meetings, I often minister by the word of knowledge. I speak things out and talk about things by the power of the Holy Spirit, and this breaks the hardness of people's hearts. You can work on a person's heart when it is hardened by telling them how much Jesus loves them. Once you start to reveal the love of God to them, their hearts will start to soften up. You must work until you break through the hard, crusty soil and get to the soft soil underneath. The hard-hearted need to know that they are accepted, loved, and forgiven; most hard-hearted people have been hurt, and they need love.

Jesus told me to take care of the people's soils, and they will start to hear the voice of God more clearly. Eventually, you will begin to hear God's voice in a greater way, but the Word of God needs to take root in your life. If you know someone who has a hardened heart, consider how you will approach them, how you will speak to them, and how you will present the love of God to them. You will need to minister to them, and sometimes you will need to fast and pray for them as well.

The Rocky Soil

The second type of soil Jesus talks about is rocky soil, which has to do with the commitment level. As Christians, we have asked Jesus Christ to come into our hearts and have walked with Him, but then some people do not want to go on. The soil is full of rocks and has no depth, and the roots of the seeds cannot take ahold. We need to be encouraged or we will not grow in the commitment level needed. When troubles come, or we are persecuted, the soil becomes rocky, and we lose our joy and fail to produce a crop. We do not want to become ineffective; we want to be able to stay in there with God.

When the soil is full of rocks, the seed cannot grow up. Under the anointing of God, you will begin to reject the rocks. You will begin to see the rocks in your life and how they were hindering you. With the help of the Holy Spirit and listening to His voice, you will remove them and triumph over them. You must get to the place where you do not blame God any longer for bad things that happen because God is not responsible for them. You will see that your commitment level needs to go to a greater height and that you need to trust the Holy Spirit and draw closer to God. Do you see how important it is to not only hear God's voice but to follow through with what He is telling you needs to change?

You also can help others with rocky soil by reminding them that they are in their Christian walk for the long run. The commitment level is for life, and no matter what, they are not going to deny Jesus Christ. You can help the rocky hearted by telling them that this is a long race, a marathon, and they need to rise to a higher commitment level and get rid of the rocks.

Jesus told me that the rocky hearted need to believe in Him, trust in Him, and get their joy back. The joy of the Lord is a healing anointing that will come in to heal them. There must be a place where there is an overcoming power in the rocky soil, and the power of God plucks the rocks out. Can you see anything in your life right now that is hindering you? Just ask the Lord to help you, and the joy the Lord will cause you to get back on track and remove those rocks. It is the joy of the Lord's healing anointing that comes in, and in these last days, you are going to see a lot more of that.

The Thorny Soil

Jesus said that many people have lives full of thorns, which represent the worries and cares of this life. Jesus told me the thorny soil represents people who are attracted to wealth and the love of money more than they are drawn to Him. You do not have to have a lot of money to be worried about money, and you can have a lot of money and still be worried about money. It is the people who are attracted to wealth, run after it, and love money who lose out in life. People with this condition of heart need to get the thorns out of the way by laying their cares down and casting them before the Lord.

> *Therefore humble yourselves under the mighty hand of God, that He may exalt you in due time, casting all your care upon Him, for He cares for you.*
>
> —1 PETER 5:6-7

A lot of the cares have to do with money problems. Satan fights Christians over money more than anything else because money is how he can control people. The enemy either gets people to seek after money or he blocks their money—either way causing them to be poor and always in need. Neither one of these conditions is good. If you let Him, Jesus will take up your cares and take care of you because He loves you. God wants to minister peace to you, and He is the One who will make everything all right. You do not need to chase money because God wants to provide for you. Seek the Kingdom of God and God's way of doing things even in the financial realm, and He will take care of you. You will receive your provision, and it will be supernatural provision from the Lord.

Is the Lord speaking to you about the soil of your heart? Do you have cares? Do you have thorns or worries in your life? Are you seeking after wealth and the love of money? Know that these are things that you will need to deal with, and the Lord wants everyone to pass their tests. What I mean by that is that God will trust you with money when *you* can be trusted. He will test you to see if you will pass tests about money.

God will speak to your heart about giving and helping other people with the money and time you have. God wants to see if you will let go of your money. If you do let go of it, more will be given, and then God will tell you where to distribute it. This testing is what happened to my wife and me. We had to learn that the money was not ours but God's, and He was giving it to us to distribute it among His people.

The Good Soil

The good soil is a heart that truly hears and receives the Word of God. Jesus said that good soil is one that produces a crop and produces thirty, sixty, or a hundredfold more than what was planted. Jesus told me that if you preach and sow the Word of God to one hundred people, only twenty would have good soil. In fact, there are four soil types, and each type represents twenty-five out of one hundred people.

Out of those twenty-five people with good soil, only about eight people would produce thirtyfold, eight would produce sixtyfold, and eight people would produce a hundredfold. That means that only eight people of the original 100 people I preached to would bring a hundredfold return, which is very low. Jesus told me that in order to see better results in Christians' lives that I had to help people heal the condition of their hearts.

He told me to address the issues of people's hearts and address their soils and then ask the Lord to come into the service as I pray for people. By the power of the Holy Spirit, I impart blessings to them and rebuke the enemy and drive out the devil. After that first initial service where I am address the condition of the soil in the people's hearts, I notice that the following services always go better.

WORSHIP

I have found that you can influence the condition of the soil of your heart when you wholeheartedly give yourself over to the Lord in worship. Picture the throne room of God as Isaiah did when he saw the Lord sitting on His throne, high and lifted up (see Isaiah 6:1-4). In the Bible, many of God's prophets saw God being worshipped in the spirit, and I picture those descriptions when I worship God. I hand myself over to Him and picture the soil of my heart being laid before the Lord, and I offer myself up. I ask the Lord to come in by His Spirit and by His power, and I prepare the soil of my heart to receive the Word of God. I think about these kinds of things as I am praying, and this is how I allow the soil of my heart to be healed.

The Lord showed me that when you worship, it is similar to the soil of your heart being in an incubator. It the atmosphere of Heaven, God starts to influence your inner man or your heart. When I am worshipping God, I see things that I did not see before, and many things are exposed by the Spirit of God. I have gotten rid of hindrances in my life just by worshipping God.

In His presence, I have realized there were certain things inside of me that were opposed to God, and I repented. You may not see it right away because there is a process that happens when you worship God. When you lay down the soil of your heart before God in worship, it is shown to you as it truly is. Then you can see clearly to take things out and repent.

You do not have to go through life with a damaged heart. There are so many people walking through this life who are hurting, and I understand that. When I was with Jesus, I did not want to come back to this broken world; I was not hurting anymore in Heaven. Then I knew that I had to come back to tell people the truth, and the truth is that you can tend to the condition of the soil of your heart. You can get the thorns and the hard ground out. You can get the rocks out, and you can start to heal. When you do, the Word of God will become more effective. You begin to receive the full benefits of the Word when you allow God to heal the soil of your heart.

A STORY

When I was with Jesus during my visitation back in 1992, He taught me so many things. One of those things was the importance of the Word of God in a believer's life. He would constantly open up spiritual truths to me during our visit. Jesus would quote Scripture continually. He would often even quote Himself! I realized that Jesus truly was the Word of God. On the other side with Him, it became so clear to me that consuming the Word of God was so necessary for our life down here on the earth. It was food that became substance inside of us and caused us to be led by the Spirit. This leading of the Spirit becomes the reason we are effective in this life as we learn to hear from our heavenly Father.

There have been many times when my wife and I would sense in our spirits to go in a certain direction and it wouldn't make sense in the natural realm, but it ended up right as we trusted the voice of God. When we lived in Seattle, we never felt to put very much money into our dream home. In fact, we felt we were not even supposed to buy a new car. It didn't make sense since we thought we would be living in our home during our later years of retirement. One day, the word of the Lord came to both of us to sell it and move to Louisiana. We left our dream home and obeyed, but it was against what we thought we wanted. Now, we realized that the Lord did not want us spending any money on that home or the car because He knew we would be moving soon.

We sold that home for a very large profit and put little into it. God is willing to lead you. You can hear His voice!

Chapter 12

LET GOD MINISTER THROUGH YOU

There are, it may be, so many kinds of voices in the world, and none of them is without signification.

—1 CORINTHIANS 14:10 KJV

THE RESULTS OF HEARING THE VOICE OF GOD involves ministry. God can speak to you and encourage you, and then you must go out and encourage and minister to others. There are a lot of voices in this world, and you can hear them in different kinds of ways. You can hear them in your psychological realm, in your physical realm, and in the spiritual realm. It is not that you cannot hear different voices; it is that some of them are not correct. There are many evil spirits and fallen beings here on the earth who operate in the spirit realm, and they will speak to you. Familiar spirits are spirits that mimic the Holy Spirit, angels, and even mimic God. Some ministers have given themselves over to familiar spirits that try to mimic God. It is supernatural, but it is not of God.

> *The spirit of a man is the lamp of the Lord,*
> *Searching all the inner depths of his heart.*
> —PROVERBS 20:27

Proverbs 20:27 is a key Scripture for me, and I keep it before me all the time. My spirit man is a lamp that is lit up by the Spirit of God. My spirit is where God speaks to me, leads me, and searches my heart. Your heart is lit up like a lamp; and as you are lit up, you encounter the anointing of God. The anointing comes upon you as it is being lit up in the depths of your heart and bears witness with what you sense in your inner man.

> *It is actually reported that there is sexual immo-*
> *rality among you, and such sexual immorality as*
> *is not even named among the Gentiles—that a*
> *man has his father's wife! And you are puffed up,*
> *and have not rather mourned, that he who has*
> *done this deed might be taken away from among*
> *you. For I indeed, as absent in body but present in*
> *spirit, have already judged (as though I were pres-*
> *ent) him who has so done this deed. In the name*
> *of our Lord Jesus Christ, when you are gathered*
> *together, along with my spirit, with the power of*
> *our Lord Jesus Christ, deliver such a one to Satan*
> *for the destruction of the flesh, that his spirit may*
> *be saved in the day of the Lord Jesus.*
> —1 CORINTHIAN 5:1-5

I want to point out here that the apostle Paul was not physically with the believers in Corinth. Paul said that he was present in *spirit* with them and that he had already judged the immoral person among them as though he was present. Paul is telling the Corinthians that when they all come together in unity by the power of the Lord Jesus Christ, Paul is also with them in the spirit. When the power of God comes, they were to turn the offender over to Satan. Profoundly, Paul is saying that he could be in one place physically and, at the same time, be in another place in the spirit.

The reason Paul wanted to turn the sexually immoral man over to Satan was that it was giving the Christians in Corinth a bad name. The voice of the Lord would never lead you to sin and be in sexual immorality as a person in the church. The Spirit of God within that man knew he was doing wrong, but the man was not able to distinguish God's voice. The man should have gotten out of that situation—or not got into it in the first place—but he found himself in bondage. Paul had to take action by telling the people to put this person out of the church. We see later in Second Corinthians 2, the man comes back into the fold because of apparent repentance.

Paul had a voice in the congregation in the Spirit, even though he was not there physically. As you meditate on God's Word and learn to walk in the power of that Word, you will start to hear God's voice. God will speak to you to become His messenger and His minister as He moves you into ministry. God is giving you a voice, and you have a voice in the spirit. Paul had a voice, and even though he was not there physically, he had a spiritual voice.

Even if you are physically unable to go somewhere, you can be in the spirit in prayer and take authority over things as Paul did. You can speak by the Spirit of God and become the voice of God for someone else. You can minister without even leaving your house. Whether physically or in the spirit, you can learn to move and walk with God to the point where God can use you to minister His voice to others. Paul became God's voice to the Corinthian church because they were not listening to God. They should have done what was right in the sight of God themselves, but they did not. So Paul had to come in and address the situation.

SPEAKING THE WILL OF GOD

You are responsible for yielding your members, your mouth, and your tongue to the Lord to minister the Word of God. When you speak the Word of God, you are speaking the will of God, and people will hear it and be rerouted. God will use you to help other people get on the right track. There are things that God needs to have addressed here on earth, and He wants to use you to do that. By His Holy Spirit, God will give you utterance, and you will speak forth by His Spirit.

I had the supernatural experience of being translated and transported in the spirit. By the power of the Holy Spirit, I have had to help fulfill God's perfect will in another person's life. I was taken way ahead in the spirit and shown the future, and I was able to reroute that person's destiny in Christ. This has happened several different times, and there are so many amazing stories.

*The voice of the Lord is over the waters; the God
of glory thunders; the Lord is over many waters.
The voice of the Lord is powerful; the voice of
the Lord is full of majesty. The voice of the Lord
breaks the cedars, yes, the Lord splinters the cedars
of Lebanon.*

—PSALM 29:3-5

I am mentioning this verse again toward the end of this book because a lot of people say that they cannot hear God's voice, and they do not know what is wrong. Here in Psalm 29, God's voice is so loud that it disrupts physical things. I tell people that they should memorize this verse and meditate on it. Jesus told me that within every person is a package that is a gift to this world and to the body of Christ. People need to become born again, and they need to come in line with God's plan for their life. The body of Christ needs to accomplish what is written about them in their books in Heaven. Your purpose and your destiny have to do with what is already written in Heaven about you. All provision and everything you need for this life has already been ordained for you before you were born.

SUPERNATURAL GIFTS WITHIN

*For the gifts and calling of God are without
repentance.*

—ROMANS 11:29 KJV

I saw that everything that you need for this life has already been provided for you. You need to start to acknowledge God in all your ways, and He will start to direct your paths (see Proverbs 3:5-6). The gifts of God are already inside of you by the Spirit of God, and they will not be recalled. The gifts and callings of God are needed so that everyone fulfills his or her destiny. The whole body of Christ depends upon you to respond to what is already within you—those things you are hearing from God. So, yield to that and give it out.

God has portioned out these gifts as the Spirit wills (see 1 Corinthians 12:11), and the Holy Spirit has gifts He manifests through people to encourage others. God also sets in the church some to be apostles, prophets, evangelists, pastors, and teachers (see Ephesians 4:11-12). These are the gifts of God that are for the governments of God. These men and women are set in the Church to bring order and to build up the body of Christ. These offices are called the five-fold ministry of the Church.

If you are called to be a prophet, then there will be certain periods of training. You must learn how to yield to the gifting of the prophet, and let God unwrap these gifts within you. You do not become a prophet right away because you have to learn how to flow in the revelatory gifts. You have to learn to flow in prophecy, and you have to learn to flow in seeing the future and knowing what you are supposed to do with the information. You will need to learn how to speak, how to operate in the gift of prophecy, the gift of healing, and the working of miracles and other giftings.

If you want to walk in authority on this earth, you will need to yield to the One who has given the authority. It is the same thing with your ministry gifts and whatever it is you are called to do. You need to walk in an intimate relationship with God, who is the Commander and Head over you. It is God who called you to be an apostle, a prophet, a pastor, a teacher, or an evangelist. It is God who calls you to prophesy, to lay hands on the sick with the gifts of healing, or to operate in the gift of miracles. God has ordained you in this life to yield to the giftings that are in you—that He Himself put in you.

You must spend time seeking God and finding out what it is God has put inside of you. You must learn to listen to the voice of God as I have taught you. Hearing God's voice is not just for you but for others. As the Holy Spirit starts to light you up and catch you on fire, then you start to minister from that fire and start to see what your giftings are. You will start to notice what kind of giftings are coming out. You will see if it is the power gifts or the revelatory gifts or the speaking gifts, and these gifts begin to develop in you. After a while, you will see that you are called to a certain office in the Church.

Some people are not called to be in a five-fold ministry of the church. You might be called to encourage people, and that is the gift of encouragement. You might have the gift of giving where God blesses you financially, and you can give as God wills. Some people are called to build houses or repair things, and you could offer your services to people and give and sow into people's lives with these gifts. I know people who are carpenters and work a job, but one day a week, they give of themselves to the body of Christ. They help people in the church and minister for free and help people who cannot afford to have things done in their houses.

Spiritually, God has placed His gifts in you, and the Holy Spirit wants to unwrap those gifts and show you what they are. The ministry that God has for you is part of your destiny in Christ Jesus, and it unfolds as you begin to yield to the voice of God. Once you begin to hear God's voice clearly, then He will start to direct you. I guarantee you that after you have had intimate fellowship with God, He will cause you to minister to others. Be encouraged that God defines your calling, and God defines your giftings. God is the One who has placed His voice within you as a born-again Christian, and *you can hear God's voice.*

A PROPHECY

The Spirit of the Lord is saying: "No longer doubt that I am with you! I am leading you with My strong right hand. You can finish your race victoriously. If you will believe and trust in Me, I will lead you into a place of rest and abundant provision. I will help you in everything you do, and you will surely hear from Me!"

You can hear the voice of God!

SALVATION PRAYER

Lord God,

I confess that I am a sinner.

I confess that I need Your Son, Jesus.

Please forgive me in His name.

Lord Jesus, I believe You died for me and that You are alive and listening to me now.

I now turn from my sins and welcome You into my heart. Come and take control of my life.

Make me the kind of person You want me to be.

Now, fill me with Your Holy Spirit who will show me how to live for You. I acknowledge You before men as my Savior and my Lord.

In Jesus' name.

Amen.

If you prayed this prayer, please contact us at info@kevinzadai.com for more information and material. Go to KevinZadai.com for other exciting ministry materials.

Join our network at **Warriornotes.tv**. Join our ministry and training school at **Warrior Notes School of Ministry**.

Visit **KevinZadai.com** for more info.

ABOUT
DR. KEVIN L. ZADAI

Kevin Zadai, Th.D., was called to ministry at the age of ten. He attended Central Bible College in Springfield, Missouri, where he received a bachelor of arts in theology. Later, he received training in missions at Rhema Bible College and a doctorate of theology from Primus University. He is currently ordained through Rev. Dr. Jesse and Rev. Dr. Cathy Duplantis.

At age thirty-one, during a routine day surgery, he found himself on the "other side of the veil" with Jesus. For forty-five minutes, the Master revealed spiritual truths before returning him to his body and assigning him to a supernatural ministry.

Kevin holds a commercial pilot license and is retired from Southwest Airlines after twenty-nine years as a flight attendant. Kevin is the founder and president of Warrior Notes School of Ministry. He and his lovely wife, Kathi, reside in New Orleans, Louisiana.

OTHER BOOKS BY KEVIN L. ZADAI

It's Rigged in Your Favor

Praying from the Heavenly Realms

Heavenly Visitation

Supernatural Finances

The Agenda of Angels

Prophetic Words for 2020

The Harrison House Vision

Proclaiming the truth and the power

of the Gospel of Jesus Christ with excellence.

Challenging Christians

to live victoriously,

grow spiritually,

know God intimately.

Harrison House

Connect with us on

f Facebook @ HarrisonHousePublishers

and 🅞 Instagram @ HarrisonHousePublishing

so you can stay up to date with news

about our books and our authors.

Visit us at **www.harrisonhouse.com**

for a complete product listing as well as

monthly specials for wholesale distribution.

Experience a personal revival!

Spirit-empowered content from today's top Christian authors delivered directly to your inbox.

Join today!
lovetoreadclub.com

Inspiring Articles
Powerful Video Teaching
Resources for Revival

Get all of this and so much more,
e-mailed to you twice weekly!

LOVE TO READ CLUB
by **D** DESTINY IMAGE